GEEK MOM

GEEK MOM

PROJECTS, TIPS, AND ADVENTURES FOR MOMS AND THEIR 21ST-CENTURY FAMILIES

Natania Barron, Kathy Ceceri,
Corrina Lawson, and Jenny Williams

ILLUSTRATIONS BY DAVE PERILLO

POTTER
CRAFT

NEW YORK

All rights reserved.
Published in the United States by Potter Craft, an imprint of the Crown Publishing Group, a division of Random House, Inc., New York.
www.pottercraft.com
www.crownpublishing.com

POTTER CRAFT and colophon is a registered trademark of Random House, Inc.

Library of Congress Cataloging-in-Publication Data
  Geek mom : projects, tips, and adventures for moms and their 21st-century families / by Natania Barron ... [et al.] ; illustrated by Dave Perillo.
—1st ed.
    p. cm.
  Includes bibliographical references and index.
  1. Home economics.   2. Parenting.   3. Handicraft.
I. Barron, Natania.
  TX145.G288 2012
  745.5–dc23   2012011924

ISBN 978-0-8230-8592-7
eISBN 978-0-8230-8593-4

Printed in the United States

Design by La Tricia Watford
Illustrations by Dave Perillo
Cover design by La Tricia Watford
Cover illustrations by Dave Perillo

10 9 8 7 6 5 4 3 2 1

First Edition

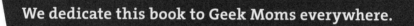
We dedicate this book to Geek Moms everywhere.

CONTENTS

FOREWORD

BY KARI BYRON
host of *MythBusters* on the
Discovery Channel and *GeekMom* columnist

When I was a kid, my dad gave me a spaceship. Not a little toy but a real, full-sized spaceship so that I could fly to the moon. At least, that is how it felt. He gave me a huge box from one of those tube televisions they had before flat screens were invented. Paint, crayons, foil, scissors, and Christmas lights made that box the coolest adventure of my fifth grade year. I ate, slept, and lived in that box. My dad taught me about space, planets, and stars. He gave me the universe. Little did I know, I had a Geek Dad.

Dad loved science fiction, *Star Trek,* and space movies. Because he loved them, I did too. Now that I am a mom, I can see my daughter following my every move the same way. I found that I can harness my love of science into crafts and projects that foster her natural curiosity and love for spending time with Mommy. She collects rocks and shells from the beach and then runs home to find them in a picture book. She is only two and a half but knows the names of the planets and has a glitter and construction-paper solar system hanging from her window. Someday I hope she will channel her geeky passions with her daughter.

As a host on *MythBusters,* I have worked in the world of geek pop culture for a decade. The best part of being on the show is the reaction I get from parents and kids. *MythBusters* inspires an excitement for science that they can share together. Becoming a mom made me understand how important that is. I had no idea how much being a MythBuster would prepare me for motherhood. All of my problem solving and love for crazy projects suited my new adventure perfectly. Just like my dad, I became part of a very special club, the Geek Moms. I realized this after I had my baby. GeekMom.com asked me to write a column for their site and I was honored. I discovered this whole new subgenre of geekdom and parenting.

Being a working mom can be hard. After a long day of blowing stuff up or crashing cars, I am sometimes devoid of creative parenting ideas. That is why I love GeekMom.com. Besides being a source of inspiration, it is also nice to see a community of moms doing what I am doing—sharing their love of geek arts with the ones they love most. Now *GeekMom* has taken their blog beyond the internet, cataloguing a wealth of great stories, experiments, crafts, projects, and activities into a book. From making a Tetris cake to dressing like a superhero to making your microwave into a science demonstration, this is the handbook for every Geek Mom.

Being a geek is being passionate about a subject (usually an esoteric one). Be it comic books, fantasy, science fiction, or technology, how amazing is it to share your passion with your kids? I feel like we are all born geeks, full of enthusiasm and wonder. If you are lucky, you don't grow out of it. I hope *Geek Mom* helps you create memories with your kids like my dad and my spaceship did for me.

INTRO

Being a geek isn't just about brains and books anymore. Being a geek is a state of mind, and that state of mind leads us to intensely explore our interests and approach the world with endless curiosity. When we want to get involved in something cool, we really get involved. In other words, we get geeky about it. And when we become mothers, we apply that same dedication and attention to detail to our parenting. We are Geek Moms.

Now, that's not to say all Geek Moms love all the same books, video games, or tech toys or are even interested in science in the same way. But we all admit to identifying in some way with being moms who want to share our love of technology, imaginative worlds, and wizardry of all types with our children. That's why we started the *GeekMom* blog in 2010 as a spin-off of Wired.com's award-winning *GeekDad* blog: as a place for geeky moms to come together to share experiences, ideas, projects, and stories, as well as to nurture the personal connections that are necessary to so many women.

With the same spirit in mind, *Geek Mom: Projects, Tips, and Adventures for Moms and Their 21st-Century Families* explores the many fun and interesting ways that moms and kids can get their geek on. With six chapters spanning everything from science to superheroes, the book contains a variety of activities and ideas that we know you will enjoy working on together, activities designed for the whole family; it even includes projects for moms to try when they get a few precious minutes alone. Every project is designed with an eye toward learning and discovery and is infused with geeky flavor, be it through pop culture, music, science, or crafts.

In and around these projects are our personal insights and suggestions about living lives as geeky parents, as well as sidebars containing added fun facts, information, and background stories about geeky women and historical moments that will hopefully keep you inspired.

But more than just a how-to, we wrote the *Geek Mom* book to encourage mothers and geeklings to be proud of their true selves. When we were growing up, being a geek meant being marginalized socially. But it's fast becoming a geek world out there, and we Geek-Moms are proud to be a large part of it!

UNDERSTANDING THE ICONS

All projects and activities have cost, time, recommended age range, and difficulty noted.

COST   TIME   AGE RANGE   DIFFICULTY

MEET THE MOMS

Natania Barron

was born in western Massachusetts in 1981, to a geeky musician dad and an artist mom. Thanks to her older cousins and encouraging parents, she got a healthy dose of video games, cartoons, Muppets, and pop culture early on. This all influenced her a great deal once she decided to become a writer (somewhere around the age of twelve or so) and perhaps helps explain her affinity for steampunk, cephalopods, and David Bowie. In college and graduate school, Natania studied the literature and history of the Middle Ages before becoming a professional business writer. She currently works in marketing by day and is a speculative fiction writer by night. Her first book, a mythpunk, world-hopping novel called *Pilgrim of the Sky*, was published in 2011; her short fiction can be found everywhere from *Weird Tales* to *Shotguns v. Cthulhu*, an anthology of Lovecraftian fiction. When not playing games or writing fiction, Natania can be found experimenting in her kitchen, strumming her guitar and ukulele, crocheting, rolling dice, watching *Downton Abbey*, and chasing after her son. She currently lives in North Carolina with her growing family. Find her at nataniabarron.com.

Corrina Lawson

is a writer, mom, geek, and superhero. She lives in rural New England with her husband, four children, and various cats. She's the author of three books in an alternate history series in which Romans and Vikings have colonized North America, *Freya's Gift, Dinah of Seneca,* and *Eagle of Seneca;* two books in her superhero Phoenix Institute romance series, *Phoenix Rising* and *Phoenix Legacy;* and the novella *Luminous.* She's currently writing a steampunk detective novel. Find her at corrina-lawson.com

Kathy Ceceri

oversees a geeky household consisting of one son who's studying electronic game design at college, another who put up a greenscreen in his room for making special-effects movies while homeschooling during high school, and an ultramarathon cyclist husband who keeps his childhood comic book collection under their bed. She has written several activity books for kids and parents, including *Robotics: Discover the Science and Technology of the Future*; contributed more than a dozen projects to the *Geek Dad* series of books; designed hands-on learning crafts for *FamilyFun, Home Education Magazine,* and others; and taught science and art workshops at museums, schools, and libraries around the Northeast. As an English major, she's especially tickled that her family's "at-home science" blogs have been mentioned in the Tech section of the *New York Times* and in *Chemical & Engineering News.* She and her family live in upstate New York. Find her at craftsforlearning.com.

Jenny Williams

was born in the 1970s, the decade where Pong was king. She grew up watching science fiction movies and TV, playing Atari, reading geeky books, solving logic puzzles, playing with computers, and doing well in school. In her teens, she discovered such wonders as BBSing, They Might Be Giants, and many more science fiction and fantasy books. Since then she has married a geek, had two of her own wickedly smart geeklings, and nurtured her many interests and passions. Currently, she thoroughly enjoys homeschooling her kids, where all her enthusiasm for learning and her variety of interests are rubbing off on them. She also spends a great deal of time writing, both personally and professionally. With what time is left, she tends to play board games with friends, and have silly but intellectual discussions. She lives in northern Arizona, happily surrounded by her own small geeky community. Find her at jennywilliams.com.

CHAPTER 1
SECRET IDENTITIES

Introduction to Imagination

My first memory of pretending to be a superhero is as a toddler when I grabbed one of my old baby blankets and fashioned it into a cape. I still remember how powerful I felt and how much fun it was. Geeky moms are in a unique position to introduce the next generation to wonder. Although superheroes are often thought of as a male bastion, it's usually mothers who first introduce their children to the concept. Mothers are generally the ones who stress out over Halloween costumes or the right books to read or the right shows to watch, and geeky mothers are the ones who pass down their love of stuff such as *Star Wars*, steampunk, fantasy, and science fiction. We're often the first to introduce children to impossible stories that fire the imagination.

The first time we show our children all the various versions of *Star Trek* and realize they love it as much as we do, it's a shared bond. The first time they come running to us about a book they just read that they love that we also loved as a child, such as *The Chronicles of Narnia,* we feel their joy. This chapter is about recapturing that feeling of exhilaration for ourselves and our children. Some of the projects are complicated, many are less so, but they are all designed with laughter and fun in mind and with an eye to providing that special thrill that pretending brings to everyone.

Why Superheroes Matter
especially to children

 It's a striking and compelling image: the ordinary-looking person sees someone around him or her in trouble and springs into action, revealing a hidden hero.

That image goes directly to our collective desire to matter, to make a difference, to be a hero. Adults are still drawn to the idea, but those who truly take it to heart are children.

Children are mostly powerless in the world. Everything around them is adult sized. They generally have no say in where they live or even where they're going on any given day. Their life is regimented. No wonder they're drawn to the fantasy of possessing incredible power under the surface.

But if superheroes were simply about power, they wouldn't speak to kids so strongly.

I asked my youngest son, age eleven, what superheroes do. He said, "They stand for justice, they fight evil guys, and sometimes they help with things like natural disasters and do stuff ordinary people can't do."

He didn't say "they have cool powers" or "they beat up bad guys" or even "they have great adventures." Instead, what he has absorbed most about superheroes is that they stand for what's right, for justice, for the best parts of humanity.

And that's why superheroes are wonderful role models for children. Not only do kids learn that they can be powerful and they can

make a difference, but they also learn the proper use of that power.

Justice is a concept that is so very hard to teach. It's not quite fairness, as kids learn early that life is not always fair. Rather, justice is about balancing the scales and trying to do the right thing, perhaps even in a bad situation. It's about being a good moral person.

This is why it's so important for superheroes to be men and women and why it's also essential for these heroes to come from as many racial and ethnic groups as possible. It's hard to adopt a superhero as a role model if he or she doesn't speak to your experience, if the hero doesn't look or act or come from the same place as you.

I was five years old when I first watched the Adam West *Batman* show in reruns. *Batman* was an ironic show that focused mainly on jokes, but it was also about the good guys trying to do the right thing. I laughed and had fun watching it, but I didn't fall in love with it until the debut of Batgirl, which hit me like a lightning bolt.

Meek librarian Barbara Gordon's wall swiveled to reveal a costume and a motorcycle. In a split second, she was transformed into a hero who could fight the villains just as well—sometimes better—than the male crime fighters.

I never, ever wanted so badly to be a superhero as on that day.

Over the years, I've absorbed other heroes beyond Batman and his supporting cast. Superman, of course, Black Canary, Green Arrow, the Justice League, the Legion of Super-Heroes, Captain America, Iron Man, the Avengers, the X-Men, and the Fantastic Four.

I learned values from all their superhero stories. Values about self-sacrifice, about morality, about the way people should treat each other.

The very first issue of the *Legion of Super-Heroes* that I ever purchased featured a reanimated soldier from the previous war intent on continuing to fight until his side achieved victory. The Legion failed to stop him in a fight and all appeared lost until the heroes looked into the soldier's background. He had originally died saving his platoon from a grenade. Once they knew this, the Legionnaires stopped the soldier by dressing as his superior officers and telling him he'd done his job well. The strange energy that had animated the soldier faded and he died knowing he'd done his job well and saved his comrades.

The Legionnaires had powers, and they were fierce fighters. But they solved the problem with intelligence and compassion instead of battle. That's what made them heroes, and that's the lesson I learned as a child.

In a story featuring Batman, the Dark Knight returned to the alley where his parents had been murdered. He had to prevent criminals from menacing an elderly woman who had once comforted the young, orphaned

Bruce Wayne on the night his parents were killed. Young Bruce had suffered, but the grown-up Bruce was now a hero who could protect others. As someone who lost her father at a young age, I took to heart the lesson that even someone who suffered a terrible loss could go on to accomplish great things.

I also took away a lasting role model for who I wanted to be like: Lois Lane. I couldn't grow up to be a superhero, but I could do what Lois Lane did. I could be a reporter. I could fight for truth as much as Superman ever did. I'm not alone. I've spoken to many female journalists over the years and a large number point to Lois Lane as their initial inspiration.

One of the very best parts of being a mother has been introducing my own children to the superheroes I loved as a child. They have had the same reaction. They love superheroes. As you can see from my son's quote earlier, they know exactly what superheroes represent: standing up for yourself, might in the service of right, and being good to each other.

An episode of *Batman: The Brave and the Bold* on Cartoon Network portrayed the sacrifice of the Doom Patrol—a band of ostracized loners—for a small number of people they didn't know. In one of the most poignant moments of Grant Morrison's *All-Star Superman,* Superman prevents a teenage girl from committing suicide. Superman knows he himself is dying from being poisoned by Lex Luthor, but he talks the girl out of jumping off a building, saying there's always a chance that life will get better.

Adults sometimes see superheroes and concentrate on the "super" part. And the costumes and the powers are a lot of fun.

But kids know better.

They know the "hero" part is far more important. They know that they can't really be superheroes when they grow up, as much as they wish they could, but they will know how to be a hero.

CREATE YOUR OWN SECRET LAIR

When I was growing up, my favorite places were the hidden ones where I could let my imagination run wild. It doesn't take special skill to create one either, just time and an old-fashioned cardboard box.

$$$
$10-$50, depending on how materials are obtained

⏱
1-2 hours (doesn't have to be consecutive)

👪
Old enough to use crayons and child paint

Easy but Mom should oversee

materials

- At least one eager child
- A large cardboard box
- A box of crayons and colored markers
- A sharp pair of scissors or a utility knife
- Glitter glue (optional)
- Stencils (optional)
- Items to decorate the interior (highly individual)

1: Finding the Materials
Appropriate-sized cardboard boxes can be found in any number of places, but I've found appliance stores are the best sources. A refrigerator box is perfect because it's the largest and roomiest, but others will do, especially if the children are younger and smaller. Several boxes can even be placed together if the kids want to expand their lair to several "rooms."

To decorate the secret lair, I recommend a big box of Crayola crayons. If the cardboard surface has been treated, try colored markers or various types of paint. Watercolors for children will work, but oil-based paints will run less, last longer, and produce more vivid images.

Use a pair of scissors or a utility knife to cut the doorways and windows into the cardboard. Please keep these, especially the knife, out of the range of small children.

2: Creating the Lair
First, consult the future owner of the lair. He or she should set the tone.

With my kids, my main job was to act

as referee if there was a disagreement and to do any tasks above their age level, such as wielding the utility knife. I have to say I didn't always do the last to their satisfaction. I received complaints if the doorways and windows were crooked. A ruler and a level are a good investment to prevent these types of comments.

Cut out the doorways and windows before any decorations or artwork are added.

After the doors and windows are done, give the children's ideas free rein. They can draw and color freehand or use stencils or rulers for neatness. Items can also be drawn on paper and then glued to the house. Glitter glue is always fun, too. But with my kids, what they wanted most was to draw or paint their own pictures onto the lair without interference.

If the kids are stumped for ideas, try suggestions such as a hidden cave, like the Batcave, the hidden rooms that appear in Hogwarts, Superman's Fortress of Solitude, a Hobbit hole, or just ask them to think of their own version of a magic room.

Remember, it doesn't have to look like a work of art when complete. It just has to feel to the child like it is his or her very own special place.

STEP 3: Move Right In!

After the exterior is done, the interior can be filled with all a child's special stuff. For my kids, this meant blankets, flashlights, various toy kitchen implements, and their favorite stuffed animals. They also wanted to sleep inside their secret lair, so that meant a sleeping bag as well. For that reason, making the secret lair in their bedroom saves moving the creation. Alternatively, it can be a special naptime place elsewhere in the house.

The only downside is that the cardboard box will fall apart at some point. That's okay, another one can always be built. Remember to take lots of photos of it, however, so the kids will remember.

TEST YOUR SUPERPOWERS

with these party ideas!

All kids (and many adults!) wish they had superpowers. Here are some quick and easy tests of strength and agility that anyone can try at home. Save them for your superhero's next get-together or party, or even a quiet afternoon. These activities are great indoors or out!

I. KIDS OF STEEL: BUILD A "TOWER" FOR YOUR SUPERHERO TO BREAK DOWN

$$\$\$			(d20 die)
$10 or less	Less than 1 hour to prepare, hours of fun	Preschool and up	Easy

materials

- Anything light and stackable, as many as possible, including:
- Plastic drinking cups (sold in large sleeves of 100–300)

- Clean, recycled cardboard milk cartons
- Empty cereal boxes (taped closed)
- Pieces of pink foam insulation (an adult can cut it into blocks and spray-paint it in stony colors)

STEP 1: Build It Up, Knock It Down

Building a wall from cups, cartons, or boxes is ridiculously easy. Just leave a small gap between each "block" as you build the first row. When you get to the second row, center each block over the gap. This technique works for straight, curved walls, and even towers. When my younger son was four, he dressed up in his Superman suit and had his dad build a tower of cups around him as high as his eyebrows to burst through. Pow!

For a party, enlist the group to build the walls as well as demolish them. With enough cups or boxes, kids can spend an entire afternoon just creating and destroying walls.

STEP 2: Clean Up and Salvage

When the kids are done building, cleanup is quick and easy. Your building materials may not survive more than one or two uses, though. If you want to save them for another superhero session, go through as you pack up to check for broken blocks to repair or recycle.

II. THE HUMAN FLY: USE CAMERA TRICKS TO "CLIMB" TALL BUILDINGS

$$\$ \$ \$$$
$10 or less

Less than 1 hour to prepare, hours of fun

Preschool and up

Easy

materials
- Flat surface that can double as the side of a building, or a roll of paper plus drawing materials
- Still or video camera
- 1 or more superheroes, appropriately dressed

STEP 1: Find, or Make, a Building Facade

This idea was inspired by the American Comic Book Heroes exhibit at the Museum of Play in Rochester, New York. The exhibit has a movie background that looks like a building turned on its side. When kids crawl along the floor, a camera turned sideways makes them look like they're scaling the building on a nearby video screen. To re-create this special effect at home, you'll need actors, a camera set at just the right angle, and a convincing background.

Use the camera's viewscreen to scout locations. Find a bare piece of sidewalk or floor that kids can crawl/climb on. A brick walkway or driveway (blocked off to traffic) is ideal. Make sure you can frame the picture to avoid any trees, grass, or furniture that can ruin the illusion.

You can add details like windows to climb past on the "building exterior" using sidewalk chalk, away from the actors, so it doesn't smear. Inside you can also use a long sheet of paper or cardboard to draw on with markers or crayons. If there's a bare wall along the floor, tape up more paper or cardboard and sketch a sideways view of other buildings going off into the distance. When your backdrop is complete and your actors are ready, it's time to set up the camera and shoot!

STEP 2: Lights, Camera, Action!

If your backdrop is the floor or ground only, position the camera operator at the foot of the climber. If you can include the wall in the shot, then turn the camera around sideways and set it at eye level with your actors. To pull off the effect, tell your stars overacting is welcome. For still pictures, have them pose in an extreme climbing position—knee bent, soles of the feet gripping the climbing surface, one hand holding on low and the other reaching way up high. If you're shooting video, have your actors move with slow, exaggerated movements. A sound track can help too, so if you've got some action film music, crank it up! Your superhero special effects will be all the more awesome!

III. ALTER THE FORCES OF THE ATMOSPHERE: CREATE A MINI TORNADO IN A BOTTLE

$10 or less

Less than 1 hour to prepare, hours of fun

Age 7 and up

Easy

materials
- Two clean, empty soda bottles, with caps
- Duct tape
- Scissors
- Water
- Food coloring, glitter, other decorations

STEP 1: Prepare the Bottles

Controlling a force of nature like a tornado is a superpower that takes great responsibility. In the right hands, however, it is both entertaining and educational. This tornado is made visible by submersing it in a bottle of water. Flip the bottle over and it spills down into the connected bottle—but it can't escape (if you make sure the connection is waterproof!).

First, fill one of the bottles two-thirds full of water. Add some drops of food coloring and glitter, confetti, or other small decorations for maximum magical effect. Then cover the opening of both bottles with duct tape so that nothing leaks out. Use the scissors to poke a small hole, about the diameter of a pencil, in the same spot on each piece of tape. Then take the empty bottle, turn it upside down on top of the water-filled bottle so the holes align, and use more duct tape to connect the two bottles firmly. The water should flow from one bottle to the other without spilling.

STEP 2: Summon the Tornado

To make the tornado appear, turn the bottles upside down so the water is on top. Hold the bottom bottle in one spot and swirl the top bottle around. The swishing of the water releases the tornado, which spirals down slowly into the lower bottle. To see it again, just turn the whole thing over and do it another time. And marvel at the power of nature!

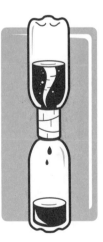

MAKE A SUPEREASY, SUPERCHEAP SUPERHERO COSTUME

My husband's a real comic book geek. One of our earliest dates was a stroll down to Forbidden Planet, the famous New York City comic book shop, to pick up the newest graphic novel in the Dark Knight series. So naturally the costume I made for our first son's first Halloween was Batman. Like most new moms, I didn't have a lot of spare time or energy—or cash—to create something elaborate. But looking at my baby's dark blue sweatpants and sweatshirt, I realized I had the basis of a great costume. And when we were done with it, it was easy to turn the costume back into wearable clothes!

Although other items of clothing can be dressed up for Halloween, sweats are versatile enough to use as the base for a range of costumes. They're easy to sew without tearing. And they're rugged and warm, which is important if late October is chilly where you live. Over the years, my kids have helped me turn sweat suits into outfits for Superman, Spider-Man, an astronaut, a medieval knight, and a Jedi. As babies, their matching tops were easy to turn into Batman (with a hooded cape) and a Dalmatian puppy. While our costumes were unmistakably homemade, the kids were always satisfied. In fact, some of their favorites never made the transition back from superhero status to normal wear but went to live in our "costume box," ready to be pulled on whenever they felt like slipping into one of their secret identities. And that was okay—our sweat-suit costumes were still worth every penny!

$10–$25

1 to 2 hours

Ages 3–4 to help plan; ages 7–8 to help cut out and sew

Easy

materials

- Sweatshirts, sweatpants, tights, and other clothing items (check both boys and girls departments for different colors)
- Felt pieces and other fabric as needed (for emblems, capes, and other details)
- Scissors, needle, and thread
- Glue or iron-on adhesive
- Fabric pens, yarn, glue-on sparkly bits, etc. (for additional details)
- Accessories (hats, boots, socks, gloves, underwear, etc.) as needed

special skills needed

Basic hand sewing

STEP 1: Assembling the Clothing Base

Look at pictures of the character you are creating to pick out the right color top and bottom. Batman gets dark blue or black, Superman a lighter blue top and bottom, and Spider-Man needs a red top and blue bottom. If you don't have a specific character in mind, go through your kids' clothes for inspiration. (A white terrycloth hooded jacket and pants my younger son owned when he was nine months old gave me the idea for the Dalmatian puppy costume.) For muscle-bound heroes like Iron Man or the Hulk, use a slightly larger size and puff it out with layers underneath. For some characters, tights make better leggings.

STEP 2: Adding the Details

For emblems and other decorations, sketch out the design on a piece of paper, then cut out layers from the appropriate colors of felt. For Batman's logo, for example, cut out an oval from black felt and the bat shape from yellow felt. Attach the layers with fabric glue or iron-on adhesive and let dry.

For one or two wearings, just baste the clothing with loose hand stitching. For my Dalmatian puppy outfit, I took a few in-and-out running stitches in each black spot, and whipstitched two floppy black ears to the hood. For rougher wear, stitch things on a little more securely. If you don't intend to reclaim the garment for everyday wear, just attach all decorations with glue or adhesive. You can also decorate permanent costumes with fabric pen, glue-on sparkles, or other special details.

STEP 3: Accessories Make the Outfit!

Adding a few clever pieces can really turn clothes into a costume. My toddler's Batman garb included a yellow felt "tool belt" that attached around his waist with Velcro closures. I shaped a piece of black fabric into a hood with bat ears that draped down to become a cape. You can also attach two pointy ears and a cape to a black winter cap that wraps around under the chin.

I attached Superman's cape right to the shoulders of the sweatshirt with a few whipstitches. Red (girls') panties and red socks over the blue tights completed the look.

Another year, my older son made a Spider-Man mask and gloves by drawing Spidey's trademark webbing using an inexpensive red knitted ski mask and gloves with black marker.

Remember, don't let your geeky penchant for accuracy take over. It's not the 501st Legion (*Star Wars* reenactors known for their professional-quality Stormtrooper costumes). The person you have to please here is your child. Repurposing everyday items into costumes is a way to introduce your kids to the joy of playing dress-up and make-believe. Your payoff will be a house full of happy superheroes to call your own.

SUPER-EASY COSTUMES FOR GIRLS

Girls can also use everyday clothing for a quick costume. Padmé from *Star Wars* just needs a white turtleneck and pants, while an adult-sized white bathrobe with a silver belt works for Princess Leia. Or use a dark blue bathrobe, white blouse, and tie for Harry Potter's pal Hermione Granger. The same robe with a gold fabric belt can be a gown for *Brave*'s Merida. Don't forget the bow!

Teaching Kids History

through the world of superheroes

 Superheroes were born at a critical juncture, in the middle of the Great Depression and just as the modern world embarked on a second world war that would forever change the future.

The first superhero, Superman, debuted in 1938 and fought corruption, standing up for the little guy, as the United States stumbled out of the Great Depression. Batman came along a year later in 1939, taking down the criminals that were too powerful for the police.

From there, the floodgates opened to all sorts of heroes, from aliens from distant planets to those who prowled the dark alleys of imaginary cities. Today, there are so many superheroes that it's impossible to name them all. But we can learn a little piece of history by studying each of them because they reflect the attitudes and pop culture of the era in which they were created.

For example, Marvel Comics published stories in the 1960s that featured a second wave of heroes relevant to that turbulent decade. Those heroes included Spider-Man, the Fantastic Four, the revived Captain America, and the Avengers. Unlike the square-jawed heroes of the past, these new heroes were more flawed and complex. Iron Man was even born in the fires of Vietnam.

Batman the television show became a campy comment on the 1960s. *Ms.* magazine put Wonder Woman on the cover of its very first issue. The world at large remembered her, even if her comic sales had sagged at that point.

It's clear superheroes, pop culture, and history are hopelessly intertwined.

I won't begin to claim that this list is all-inclusive. It's far more a list of places to start. The recommended books each cover a critical time period or issue and each can be used as a teaching tool for anyone eager to see history through the prism of tights, capes, and superpowers.

Suggested Reading:

- The late 1930s to the 1950s: *Superman Chronicles,* by Jerry Siegel, beginning with volume 1; *The DC Vault: A Museum-in-a-Book with Rare Collectibles from the DC Universe* by Martin Pasko; and *The Marvel Vault: A Museum-in-a-Book with Rare Collectibles from the World of Marvel* by Roy Thomas and Peter Sanderson (this could be hard to find, as it's out of print).
- For the 1940s to the present day: Feminism from the original Wonder Woman to

Lois Lane to Birds of Prey. *The Wonder Woman Chronicles,* vol. 1, by William Moulton Marston; *Superman's Girlfriend, Lois Lane Archives,* vol. 1; *DC Comics Covergirls* by Louise Simonson; and *Birds of Prey: Sensei & Student* by Gail Simone.

- World War II: *The Sgt. Rock Archives,* vol. 1, by Robert Kanigher.
- Batman and the rise of the urban crime fighter from 1939 to the present day: *Batman Chronicles,* vol. 1, by Bill Finger and Bob Kane; *Batman in the Seventies* by Dennis O'Neil; and *Batman Incorporated,* vol. 1, by Grant Morrison.
- The McCarthy era and blacklisting through *JSA: The Golden Age* by James Robinson.
- The groovin' 1960s through the eyes of Bob Haney's *The Silver Age Teen Titans Archives,* vol. 1.
- The space program and scientific exploration in Fantastic Four: *Fantastic Four,* vol. 1, by Stan Lee.
- The Cold War through the eyes of Marvel's secret agent Nick Fury: *Nick Fury, Agent of S.H.I.E.L.D.* by Jim Steranko.
- The 1970s and disillusionment with Captain America: *Captain America: Nomad (Avengers)* by Steve Englehart.
- The African American experience in comics: individual issues of *Black Lightning* by Tony Isabella; and *Icon: A Hero's Welcome* by Dwayne McDuffie and M. D. Bright.
- For all eras: *Batman: The Brave and the Bold,* an animated TV series to be watched while holding *The DC Comics Encyclopedia* as supporting text.

A Quick Guide to Each Era

The first step in teaching history through superheroes is deciding where to begin. Some of the recommended titles won't be suitable for all ages, and others might not coincide with the child's interests.

I'm not big on forcing a child to study, and I designed the list of books above as either a formal course guide or as a handy reference for when those teachable moments arrive unexpectedly. While I've listed the eras chronologically, they certainly don't have to be introduced that way.

For the youngest children, I'd start with the DC and Marvel Vaults because they have cool reproductions of products and gadgets offered either with the comics or as part of the promotion of DC Comics over the years. They're great pieces of bygone pop culture and can start many discussions with kids. Plus, they're tactile. Kids love to touch things.

On the feminism list, I believe any girl growing up would have fun learning how the women's roles have changed through the years by viewing them through the lens of comics. *DC Cover Girls* offers some eye-popping (and often funny) visuals—particularly the *Superman's Girlfriend, Lois Lane* covers—for younger children who might not be ready for the comic stories. The early Wonder Woman comics and their reliance on bondage may raise some parents' eyebrows but will go over the heads of younger children. *Birds of Prey: Sensei & Student* is the book both my daughters loved and that I used as a gateway into modern-day superheroes for them.

The Sgt. Rock tales from World War II actually cover two eras, the one in which they're set as well as Korea and Vietnam.

Rock first appears in 1959. That means while his stories take place in World War II, the sensibilities concerning the cost of war are from a later era, much like the television show *M.A.S.H.* was set in Korea but was more of a commentary on Vietnam.

Batman is fascinating to track because he's one of the heroes who changed the most over time. At first, he was a dark avenger of the night, bringing order to chaos. By the time the 1960s ended, he'd been demystified as part of the popular television show. But he was brought back to his more realistic roots in the 1970s and became progressively grimmer and darker until expanding in the present day to *Batman Incorporated.*

JSA: The Golden Age features many of the forgotten Golden Age heroes of DC comics coming to grips with the world in which their heroism seems to be no longer needed.

It's inspired by the real-life McCarthy-era investigations, much as the same events inspired Arthur Miller's play *The Crucible.* I happen to think *JSA: The Golden Age* is a lot more fun to read, however, than Miller's play. For one, more battle sequences.

The 1960s were a time of incredible output for Marvel Comics' Stan Lee and Jack Kirby, and the Fantastic Four is one of their most enduring creations. From the beginning, the Four were all about exploration, into space or other dimensions or even in the earth below. It's fun to read the early comics and talk with kids about what's still correct scientifically and what still holds true.

For pure silliness, Bob Haney's *Teen Titans* cannot be missed. Haney was not of the hippie generation, but he tried to write as if he were and the resulting adventures not only spotlight the issues of the day but also are so over the top they're a blast to read with the kids.

Nick Fury, Agent of S.H.I.E.L.D., by Jim Steranko, is the gold standard for superhero spy comics as Steranko's incredible visuals not only take Fury through the Cold War but also deal with supervillain secret societies that our real world never had to fight.

Captain America is, like Batman, a touchstone for how heroes change with the times. In the early 1970s, as America went through a loss of innocence with Watergate, so did the comic book hero who proudly wore the flag. The Englehart stories are a great way to introduce children to the idea that governments can be flawed because people are flawed. But Cap never loses hope in America or its people.

Minorities weren't always well represented in the comic world. Marvel did better with the introduction of Black Panther and Luke Cage, Power Man—though he was somewhat over the top—but the first African

American hero I absolutely adored was Jefferson Pierce, Black Lightning, a star scholar and Olympic gold medalist who came to an inner-city school to teach. Sadly, his short series isn't collected in trade. The Milestone line of comics came out over a decade later, in 1993, as a branch of DC comics. The entire line was devoted to African American heroes such as Icon, that universe's version of Superman. Milestone also gave birth to Static, the star of the *Static Shock* cartoon series.

The *Batman: The Brave and the Bold* show on Cartoon Network served as a great jumping-on point for discussing comic history with my kids, as it featured forgotten heroes from previous eras, like B'Wana Beast and the Doom Patrol. I used *The DC Comics Encyclopedia* to answer all their questions, which tended to lead to more questions, which tended to lead me to finding comic book collections they requested.

That meant they had more material to read, always a win.

Recommended Superhero Comics for Children

This list, created with the input of the four younger experts in my house, spotlights the best superhero titles for children (and their parents). Of course, these are not the only superhero books kids will enjoy, but it is a place to start.

FOR YOUNGER READERS, PRESCHOOL TO AGE SEVEN:
Ultimate Spider-Man by Brian M. Bendis and Mark Bagley: The best place to begin for new readers of Spider-Man. The ultimate universe features a teenage Peter Parker reimagined for modern times. The first series ran for 160 issues until Peter tragically died. Now Miles Morales, a middle-school student, is the new Spider-Man. My children pronounced this "awesome."

The Batman Adventures and The Gotham Adventures, various creators: A spin-off of the popular *Batman: The Animated Series* show from the 1990s, this Batman is great for children, and it's the version I often prefer. Easy-to-follow art makes the story readable even for the youngest children.

Marvel Adventures Avengers, various creators: The *Marvel Adventures* line is designed for younger readers and features all the familiar Marvel characters in readily accessible and age-appropriate stories. The tales are charming and wonderful. Familiar characters include Captain America, Thor, Iron Man, Hulk, and many others.

Crisis on Multiple Earths, DC Comics, various creators: As a child reading comics off the spinner racks, the annual DC crossovers between the Justice League of America on Earth-1 and the Justice Society of America on Earth-2 were a special treat. Those stories are now available in several collected volumes and feature all the familiar heroes. The emphasis on action and visuals is perfect for younger readers.

AGES SEVEN TO ADULT:
Crisis on Infinite Earths by Marv Wolfman and George Perez: The mega-crossover that changed the whole setup of the DC comics universe collected in

one huge volume. It's filled with practically every character who ever appeared in DC Comics, incredible art by illustrator George Perez, and the story, though vast, is easy to follow.

Blue Beetle by John Rogers, Keith Giffin, and Cully Hamner: After another universe-altering crisis, teenager Jaime Reyes became the new Blue Beetle by virtue of an alien tech device. Jaime has an excellent supporting cast, most prominently his friends and family, and my kids were hooked on the title. Jaime's also appeared a number of times on the cartoon series *Batman: The Brave and the Bold,* so children who watched him on that will love this book.

Runaways by Brian K. Vaughn, various artists: The very first Marvel comic my teenage daughter loved. It has a simple premise: their parents are supervillains so the kids band together to stop them. It's all about friendship and loyalty.

The New Teen Titans Archives by Marv Wolfman and George Perez: The book where Robin becomes Nightwing, where Starfire and Raven were first introduced, and where Deathstroke became a villain for the ages. The *Teen Titans* cartoon series drew heavily from the stories in this comic.

YOUNG ADULT READERS, FOURTEEN AND UP:
The Sandman by Neil Gaiman:
The only comic series that I've ever convinced my English literature major husband to read. Gaiman's stories were acclaimed when they were published two decades ago and they hold up today. This story is about the power of dreams, hope, and the humaneness to be found even in those who are immortal. Parental warning: There are definite adult sensibilities in this series, so read before handing it over to younger kids.

DC: The New Frontier by Darwyn Cooke: When people ask me why I love superheroes, I hand them this book. It's a reimagining of what the DC heroes—Superman, Batman, Flash, Green Lantern, Martian Manhunter—would be like if they first appeared in the 1950s. The story takes the heroes through a mostly dark and suspicious era until ultimately providing hope with the dawn of the New Frontier in the 1960s.

Catwoman by Ed Brubaker, various artists: *Catwoman* was relaunched in 2001 with a redesign by Darwyn Cooke and Ed Brubaker. The noir-inspired series introduced Selina Kyle as a protector (in her own antihero way). Definitely not for children, as it features R-rated sex and violence.

Secret Six by Gail Simone, various artists: The Secret Six are a group of villains who are bound together by a feeling that they won't be accepted by anyone else.

The Comic Books Under the Bed

living with someone else's obsession

 Geeks are known for their obsessions and quirks—but not their flexibility. So when two geeks get together and start a family, disagreements are bound to come up. Just when you've reached the stage in life where you can finally have everything just the way you like it, someone else comes along with their own strongly held views. Adjusting can be hard. But to preserve your relationship, it's best to learn how to put up with your mate's own geeky tendencies.

Not all Geek Moms are married to Geek Dads. And Geek Dad-ism, like many things, exists on a continuum from "enjoyed the first *Star Wars* movie" to "named his first daughter Leia." My husband falls somewhere in between: he convinced me a theme park would be the perfect honeymoon spot, and he decorates our Christmas tree each year with *Star Trek* ornaments. More than once I've walked into the dining room to find the table covered with a computer broken down into all its component parts. But he isn't a fanatic about the latest technology—in fact, his cell phone is only good for making calls, he pays our bills by snail mail, and (gasp) he doesn't own a single Apple device.

On the other hand, there are the comic books. I knew when I married him that among the property he brought to our union was a comics collection he'd started in junior high. We joked that the trunkful of first issues in his mother's attic was our kids' college fund. Then one day, I came home to find our bed up on stilts, and half a dozen long white cardboard boxes filled with comic books arranged neatly underneath.

Now, our decorating style is definitely eclectic. My husband has never complained about the stuffed Hedwig and Golden Snitch on the bookshelf over the sofa. He's never suggested I get rid of the crystal radio antenna wire that runs from the mudroom, across the kitchen ceiling, up the stairs along the banister, and into the master bedroom (where it hwangs across the curtain rods). And I had managed to accept the Miss Piggy bank (the one with the slot for coins in her cleavage) and the Tigger doll he got at Disney World when he was eight that sit on the shelf next to his side of the bed.

But raising the bed up another six inches on plastic risers to stuff comic book boxes underneath seemed to be crossing the line. It wasn't that I begrudged him his special interest—but did it have to live under our bed?

I have to say that suppressing the urge to throw a fit over my new bedroom decor was not easy. But in the end, I figured that resistance was futile. After all, he graciously puts up with—and sometimes even encourages—my own quirky interests. And as my husband has shown many times over the years, geeks who treasure their childhood mementos so dearly make really great dads.

But perhaps most important, without our geeky spouses and their maddening quirks, what would there be to blog about on the internet?

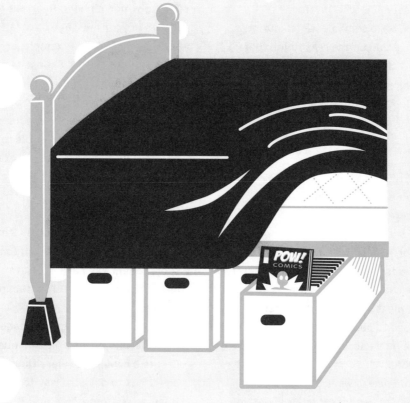

SECRET AGENT MAN

following clues in your own treasure hunt

If you want to hide a secret message, a birthday present, or a prize of some kind for your kids or loved ones, creating your own treasure hunt is a fun way to do so. This works equally well for kids and grown-ups; just create the clues using the appropriate difficulty level. Your secret agent, no matter his or her age, will enjoy the challenge of solving puzzles and finding hidden treasure.

Throughout history, people have sent messages by secret code, whether to mask their behavior, or to send messages during wartime. Depending on the reason for your treasure hunt, choosing a theme for the clues makes it even more fun. Theme ideas include being a spy during wartime, finding "buried" pirate treasure, or sending secret notes among friends.

STEP 1: Create Secret Clues

Choose what kind of clues you would like to create. You might want to follow a theme, with a unifying thread running throughout, or you might want a variety of different puzzles. If you choose to use secret codes for the clues, make sure the recipient of the secret message knows what method they should use to decode them. For children, giving them a mini decoder book at the start would be helpful.

There are endless ways to encode your messages, but these suggestions will get you started.

Secret codes:

- Transposition ciphers: Rearrange the letters in your message to create a scrambled code, for example, anagrams.
- Substitution ciphers: For each letter or character in the original message, substitute a different character, or even a symbol or sound, for example, Morse code.
- Symbols: Use special symbols to mean different letters or words, for example, semaphore flags or sign language.

Other ideas for clues:

- Use invisible writing, such as lemon juice on paper, to hide the message. The secret agent will have to figure out what needs to be done to reveal the message, such as applying heat.
- Write clues in a foreign language, with Greek letters, or with Roman numerals.
- Create a challenge where the secret agent has to devise a way to get something down from a tree or untangled from a rope.

Free to as much as
you'd like to spend

Hunt creation,
30-90 minutes

Age 5 and up

Easy

materials

- Clue containers (e.g., plastic Easter eggs, prescription pill bottles, aluminum pill containers, Altoids tins, Hide-a-Key magnetic containers, snack baggies)
- Paper and pen for writing clues
- Books or reference material for secret code ideas
- Treasure chest or other special final container
- Small prizes for final container (e.g., polyhedral dice; wax-covered string; small games, such as card or dice games; books; candy that won't melt in the sun)
- Notebook, and pen or pencil for the secret agent

- Use GPS coordinates as a clue and have the secret agent find the location with a GPS device.
- Give your secret agent a compass, and have the clues guide them a certain number of steps in a cardinal direction.

Tips:

- Control the difficulty by either having all the hidden clue containers look the same, or by having all of them look different.
- Vary the hiding places. Don't have all the clues in bushes, or behind trees, or under rocks.
- It may help to number the clues to keep them straight during planning.
- Most important: When generating the clues, work backward! Decide first where you want the final container to be placed, and then work backward from there, deciding on hiding places first and then creating clues to point to those hiding places. That way, you are always done with the treasure hunt if you need to be, or you can keep adding more and more clues to make it longer.

STEP 2: Hide the Clues

Once you have chosen all your clues and hiding places, fill the containers and hide them in their designated locations while your secret agent is otherwise occupied. Don't place the clues too far in advance, or weather or curious onlookers may interfere.

STEP 3: Hold the Treasure Hunt

When the time comes, hand the secret agents the first clue, their notebooks, and their pens or pencils, and stand back and watch. Some clues may turn out to be easier or more difficult than you originally thought. Be sure to give your secret agents the time they need to figure the clues out on their own, but also know when to step in to give gentle hints, depending on their age and how easily frustrated they are. Once your secret agents reach the final clue, congratulate them. They have completed their mission!

STEP 4: Hold a Postmortem

Depending on your audience, some parts of the treasure hunt may have worked better than others. Talk about the successes and failures, what was particularly fun and what may have been a drag, and what to change or add for next time. Encourage your kids to share their perspective, and also to create treasure hunts for each other, or for you, in the future!

Steampunk and Maker Culture

 There is virtually no agreement about exactly when steampunk began. Some cite H. G. Wells and Jules Verne; others claim it simply emerged full-fledged from the ether in a flurry of petticoats and monocles. Whatever the beginning, we can attribute the term, at least, to K. W. Jeter, who used it in a letter to *Locus* magazine in April 1987. Think of steampunk as the imagined future of a Victorian past, if you will. Cogs, brass, corsets, goggles, airships, and pistols.

Steampunk has not only grown into a magnificent subgenre of fantasy and science fiction, spawning works by authors such as China Miéville, Cherie Priest, and Scott Westerfeld, it has also given rise to a culture of costumers, tinkerers, and makers. You need not go much further than any given Maker Faire to note these curious geeks bedecked in the fashion of the Victorian period, albeit with their own twist.

While steampunk literature reimagines a possible future for the Victorians, steampunk makers live it. From music to technology, today's steampunk dabbles in many subcultures, and some theorize it even sprang forth from the Goth movement of the 1990s. Whether it's a hand-tooled leather corset, a pair of goggles, or a refashioned computer case, the steampunk aesthetic has hit hard, and it is quickly finding its way to the masses.

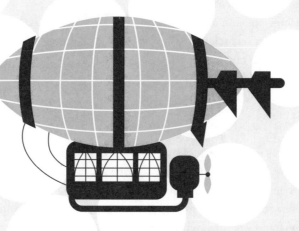

THE THRIFTY STEAMPUNK COSTUME

Although recent steampunk fashion may have taken a turn for the commercial, its roots are firmly rooted in maker culture and, by extension, the thrift store. My mom started me off in thrift stores when I was in junior high, where I could find amusing additions to my wardrobe that were one of a kind. So it's no surprise that I fell in love with steampunk costuming and the hands-on nature of its design.

There really is no hard-and-fast rule as to what is and what isn't steampunk. Most people go for a vaguely Victorian look (except, you know, with the ladies wearing corsets outside their clothing rather than under). Some people make the mistake of thinking that steampunk is all about brown (as Jess Nevins famously quoted: "Steampunk is what happens when Goths discover brown"), but there's no need to be stymied by a single color. In fact, the Victorians loved all sorts of audacious colors and patterns, fabric choices, and unusual hats. Leaf through some old *Harper's Bazaar* magazines from the late nineteenth century and you'll see what I mean.

The thrift store is an ideal place for collecting cheap items for your costume. Not only is it affordable, but it's eco-friendly and far more fun than buying something out of the box. And that's not to mention that your creation will be unique and won't even require the use of a sewing machine (though I've found glue guns to be useful, if not exactly period, from time to time).

STEP 1: For Steampunks of All Ages, Start with the Basics

A white cotton blouse or a cotton shirt is a great place to begin, whether you're going for an airship pirate or a Victorian lady about town. A comfortable (and cheap!) base will go a long way.

STEP 2: Find the Leather Belts, Seriously

Look for riveted belts, tooled belts, interesting belts. Layer them, loop them. You'll be surprised how far they'll go!

STEP 3: Think in Layers

Multiple shirts. Vests over corsets. Gloves, cuffs, and so on. I think some of the best steampunk costumes I've seen out there simply look lived in, and layering different materials and patterns really helps to achieve the look.

STEP 4: Go Beyond the Clothing Aisle

Visit homewares, pick up cloth remnants. Bits of machinery, old rusty lanterns, belt buckles, badges, birdcages: all these things can be refashioned into part of the story of your costume. Though you don't have to think of a theme, having one can help you (or your younger, easily distracted geeklet) stay focused. If you don't like the color of something, don't fret: there's always metallic spray paint.

STEP 5: Experiment

Half my costumes have been hacked together with one central piece (like a corset) and lots of other rotating pieces: scarves, hats, shawls, shoes, jewelry. Steampunk is all about the expression of the individual, but it's also about getting a good bang for your buck. Look to a variety of inspirations, from the Wild West to the Near East, and you'll never be at a loss! And remember: goggles are a suggestion, not a requirement!

Steampunk themes are all about the details: add a mustache and a hat for a steampunk cowboy; a monocle and top hat with some well-placed gears makes a gentleman or gentlelady inventor; or go classic with the airship pilot—all you need is a pair of goggles, a long scarf, and some fun pins!

THE ADVENTURES OF THE THRIFT STORE KID

Thrifting came to me out of necessity, but it never felt like that. I owe it entirely to my mother, who is nothing if she is not a thrift store geek. I can't tell you when I started going to thrift stores because I can't recall a time where it wasn't a part of our lives. My mom inherited her mother's eye for high-quality clothing and jewelry, and coupled with her amazing fashion sense (typically out of the influence of trends), she's always looked like a starlet without having to break the budget. Not to mention that she made every trip to Goodwill feel like an adventure.

While I'll admit to having a penchant for buying '70s fare in high school (bell-bottoms, dashikis, and even velvet shirts), I've learned more about history at thrift stores than anything. By now I can recognize various Spode pottery patterns, can spot sterling silver at twenty paces, and can pick out a designer purse in a pile of bags.

The thing is, thrift stores are remarkable history lessons. It's not just about buying stuff. Sure, finding that perfect A-line dress that makes you look like an extra from *Mad Men* is absolutely a thrill. But I've found,

throughout many years of perusing the aisles, that looking is just as important. Thrift stores are filled with learning opportunities. Take your kids, and have them guess what various things are (a box for tapes? an over-the-fire popcorn popper? a mustache mug?). Use the opportunity to talk to them about how things have changed, or make up the history of something that baffles all of you.

With a little research, and a little imagination, you, too, can find adventures in any thrift store!

BUDGET RENAISSANCE CORSET

(just for mom)

This project was inspired by a trip to a local art store during one of the most financially challenged periods in our life. It was nearing time for our local Renaissance Faire, and I was sadly going to attend without the appropriate attire. Then I spied a bamboo mat used for wrapping up paintbrushes and realized I had a handful of similar ones at home that I used for placemats. Their size and shape would be ideal to use as boning in a corset pattern, especially considering how expensive bone, plastic, or metal busks are (often the most expensive part of a corset). Coupled with the fact that I owned a good few yards of thick muslin, some lovely tartan material, and everything else save the ribbon, I was able to create a corset for around $15.

$$$

Varies, depending on materials at hand

Dependent on level of detail desired

Adult

Advanced

materials

- Bamboo mats (3 will do)
- Sturdy tape (electrical or duct)
- Material as dictated by your scrap stash and/or desire (as per corset instructions, consult the list)
- Sewing machine (unless you're going truly authentic)

STEP 1: Gather Your Materials

This is a flexible project, and I am no seamstress by nature. I've made two corsets using the generator and instructions over at The Elizabethan Costume (their generator is at elizabethancostume.net/custompat, and instructions and more details are at elizabethancostume.net/corsets), and I can't recommend it enough. I would not suggest bamboo for anything other than a Renaissance corset, because bamboo is generally stiff and works best on the straight lines.

STEP 2: Disassemble a Handful of Bamboo Placemats

This can easily be done by snipping the string that typically holds them together.

STEP 3: Collect the Reeds

Collect them in groups of about three or four until you have enough to slip into the corset channels. You're looking for a cluster the size of a narrow pencil, or a little narrower. For the busks (hardier boning used near the lacing) I used flat bamboo that happened to come with my mat, but if you don't have that you can always double up. Tape each cluster in the middle and cut to size according to your measurements (you may need a Dremel tool for this: bamboo is tough stuff).

STEP 4: Cover the Ends

Tape the tops and bottoms of the cut reeds. This is essential as, otherwise, while you move the individual reeds will move about and poke through!

STEP 5: Insert the Boning

Slide the bamboo "boning" down into the channel and finish corset as pattern indicated (typically this is one of the last steps before finishing the seam).

Whether you're going for brocade and silk or muslin and tartan, it doesn't matter. What's cool about bamboo is that it's surprisingly period, since the Elizabethans used dried reeds in their corsets. Having worn this style corset, complete with bamboo, a few times now, I can attest to its strength and support.

EDITH HEAD:
COSTUME DESIGNER AND INSPIRATION TO MANY

Name: Edith Head // **Lived:** October 28, 1897–October 24, 1981 //
Occupation: Costume designer // **Known for:** Her distinctive personal look

Famous costume designer to the stars, Edith Head had to be very clever to get herself into the movie industry at the start. She held a master's degree in French from Stanford University and soon found employment teaching French, but she was also able to talk her way into teaching art, despite having little background in the subject. She took art classes on the side to get up to speed, and this knowledge and experience landed her a job as a costume sketch artist at Paramount Pictures in 1924, securing her place in American movie history.

Many of the other costume designers working at the time were male, so Edith was already an anomaly. But her style of working and her consultations with the female stars, which the men rarely did, set her apart. This made her a favorite designer among many of the leading ladies of the 1940s and 1950s, including such actresses as Bette Davis,

Grace Kelly, and Audrey Hepburn. She was so popular that the studio often had to lend her out at the request of actresses doing films for other studios. She also worked frequently on Alfred Hitchcock films.

Edith designed many costumes that were more timeless and less tied to fads, because of Paramount's policy

of not wanting their films to appear dated. She became the head designer at Paramount after being there for fifteen years and stayed with that studio for a total of thirty years. She later moved to Universal Studios, where she remained for the rest of her life.

Edith worked on more than eleven hundred films during her career, and she was nominated for thirty-five Academy Awards, winning eight times, more than any other woman. In a world previously dominated by men, Edith's boldness and capability allowed her to become possibly the greatest costume designer in the movie industry.

Later in the 1960s, she wrote a book called *How to Dress for Success*, containing all kinds of sketches of fashion dos and don'ts for different situations, such as when you want to get a job, or get a man, or balance an outfit and add accessories. However, the book was full of useful quotations from her as well, giving wisdom on much more than just fashion.

Lest you think she only did fashionable costumes for movie stars, in the mid-1970s she also designed United States Coast Guard uniforms for women. She even received an award for this assignment.

Edith's last film was *Dead Men Don't Wear Plaid*, with Steve Martin. She was called on to re-create fashions from the 1940s with plenty of film noir references. She now has a star on the Hollywood Walk of Fame.

Even today, Edith Head is still with us in spirit. She was featured on a stamp in February 2003 from the US Postal Service. The stamp series focused on those who worked behind the scenes in filmmaking. They Might Be Giants also put out a song called "She Thinks She's Edith Head." And of course, the character Edna Mode from the movie *The Incredibles* shows more than a passing resemblance to Edith. Though the film's director has neither confirmed nor denied the resemblance, it is pretty obvious to me that Edna is a cartoon version of Edith Head.

Fans, Conventions, and Costuming

navigating the throng together

There is no doubt that conventions have become one of the cornerstones of geek society. It doesn't matter if you're a **Who** geek or a **Trek** geek or a **Craft** geek or a **Tech** geek, there is inevitably a convention to suit you somewhere. Conventions don't just serve as great places to learn about one's geek flavor-of-the-week (or dabble in flavors never before sampled), but they're also wonderful places for meeting other geeks. In fact, through conventions, I've managed to meet Corrina, Kathy, and Jenny (at Pax East in Boston and Maker Faire in San Matteo, California). Beyond meeting folks you may only know in the virtual world and those you never knew existed, conventions are a veritable smorgasbord of geekery, a place to downright marinate in games, kitsch, and the culture.

But how do kids fit in? Admittedly, this is not a question with an easy answer. A quick visit to any convention, large or small, will demonstrate a wide variety of approaches to integrating children into a convention setting. That is, some do and some don't. I've heard of couples hiring nannies to watch their kids at night; I've seen babies in pouches hauled through Dragon*Con in full-out Yoda costume; and I've spoken to parents who've left their kids at home and are enjoying a weekend out on their own.

No matter how you cut it, having kids makes convention going more challenging than doing so while unhindered. It means planning in advance. It means setting realistic goals. And perhaps more than anything, it's about asking yourself what you want out of

a convention. If it's a romantic escape you're looking for, hauling around kids might not be a good idea. Looking for a family outing? You might want to make sure the convention is family friendly, especially when it comes to younger kids. Believe it or not, some conventions even have day care, provided you get on the list early enough. But many conventions simply aren't meant to cater to kids, and parents should do plenty of research before bringing the entire brood.

Fans

Many geeks are fans by nature, and they are willing to drive/fly/hitchhike/TARDIS anywhere to get in close proximity to their favorite actors and actresses. But be aware, once your kids are old enough to develop their own fandoms, they may request conflicting panels and signings. Never thought you'd be standing in line for six hours to get the autograph of Tom Kenny, the voice of SpongeBob, did you?

If you're married, or traveling with a group, make sure you plan ahead—and involve your kids in the discussion. Tag-team various panels if necessary with younger kids, and strive to meet up at specific points with older kids and teens who can navigate the convention on their own. Kids have become so essential to conventions these days that many have entire tracks dedicated to the younger set.

Yes, all this keeping tabs and planning likely means you'll have to compromise a bit. You'll probably have to sit through a handful of panels that you have virtually no interest in. But getting your kids comfortable in a convention environment and supporting their own fandom is superimportant if you want them to be enthusiastic, well-informed, fun-loving conventiongoers. Remember, not everyone's idea of a great time is a seven-hour dungeon crawl in the basement of the Hilton.

Conventions

A little planning goes a long way. In our family, we decided to take our son first to a small, in-state convention. It was a science fiction convention in a small hotel at which I was a guest panelist. While I was in panels, my husband took the helm, walking around to get our son familiar with the lay of the land and introduce him to the magic of the vendor halls. The highlight of his visit was getting two Hot Wheels carrying cases filled to brimming with cars for a mere $10. Yes, a good association, even if his fandom isn't ours.

If you are taking your kids, listen to them. Seek out conventions that will have plenty for them to do, but make sure you've got enough to keep you satisfied. It's a balance. If your kids are extrasensitive or introverted, it might not be best to start them with a huge convention unless you're certain they'll have access to quiet spots (believe you me, even some "private" hotel rooms are far from quiet in a convention setting). Even if you aren't taking your kids, be aware that you'll likely be far more exhausted than you remember after your weekend away. Schedule a day or two on either side of your trip to recuperate and get back in the groove.

Costuming

What about costuming? It's likely that, with the addition of geeklets in the household, you might not have the same kind of time to devote to your costume as you might have had in previous years. Gone are the hand-sewn sequins and custom finishes. And you might as well give up hopes of a coordinated family costume, unless your kids are really compliant. More often than not, kids have entirely different ideas of what they want to wear (if anything at all) to a costume-centric convention.

Keeping it simple will help in the long run. Rather than aspiring for costumes that require tons of handmade details, consider something a little more open-ended, like a steampunk costume or a Captain Mal costume. Many recognizable characters can be put together with a little help from your thrift store with no problem at all. Enlist your kids to help. Brainstorm the elements of the costume you're looking to assemble well before the convention and work together. Be realistic, but don't miss out on the opportunity to splurge on a few really awesome showcase pieces that might convey across years (or as hand-me-downs).

Whatever your approach, conventions can be a rewarding and absolutely memorable family experience. Just make sure what your definitions of "rewarding" and "memorable" are before you head out—and be sure to prepare yourselves for surprises. You never know what might happen!

KIDS AND COSTUMES

Every kid is different. Some moms expect their kids to be into costumes the moment they can distinguish pants and shirts from one another and end up with kids who couldn't care less. Others are taken aback by their kids' desires to turn anything into a cape or a skirt.

Whatever the case, it's important that you let your kid take the lead. Sure, it's all within reason. Not every parent has the time or the resources to meet their kid's every whim. But allowing children enough room to contribute to the decision process and tapping in to their natural energy and imagination will always garner the best results.

So speaks the mother of the four-year-old who wanted to be a steampunk poodle for Halloween. And you know what? He looked great in the end.

CHAPTER 2
ELEMENTARY, MY DEAR WATSON

A Child's Natural Sense of Curiosity Will Lead the Way into Learning

Children see the world differently than adults do. Everything is new to them. They are open to more possibilities, and their minds aren't yet preprogrammed from experience and external pressure about how to make choices. This chapter is about carefully harnessing children's sense of wonder and natural curiosity to both educate them and enhance our own understanding of the world.

Unlike us, kids don't have jobs, to-do lists, or housekeeping as distractions. They're able to give their full attention to whatever they concentrate on. By noticing what they notice, when they notice it, and why they notice it, parents can nudge children toward learning in the course of an ordinary day while doing seemingly ordinary things.

To add to your existing repertoire, this chapter includes educational activities, projects, and information that will help inject fun and new understanding into your family's day. They will be having fun while they learn, which is the easiest and most successful way to foster lifelong learning.

Education is something that happens all the time. It doesn't need to be reserved for the hours that kids are in school, and the option of homeschooling offers an even more flexible environment for learning, for the entire family at once. Make informal learning and education an integral part of life, and your kids will take the initiative to explore new subjects and ideas. Helping your kids learn doesn't take special skills, and you don't even have to be a geek to take advantage of this willingness to learn. It simply takes paying attention to your children, especially when they ask, "Why?"

Organize a Home Learning Center

Learning can take place anywhere in the house. And you don't need special equipment. Send your kids out in the yard with a garden hose and a bucket and they can probably learn a month's worth of classroom science in an afternoon. Of course, most geek households have enough books, videos, and media devices to give kids access to all the information they could ever need. But if you really want to encourage learning at home, it helps to have a variety of tools and materials on hand that are easy for kids to get to on their own. As homeschoolers know, some of the best kinds of education occur when children are left alone to pursue their passions and sudden inspirations.

If you've got a spare room or workspace to set aside for your kids, you can create a dedicated home learning center. Having a place where kids can get messy without worrying about ruining the furniture, and where they can leave out half-finished projects to work on another day, is ideal. But even in smaller homes like mine, you can still store quite a lot of educational tools if you commandeer a shelf here and a drawer there. Depending on the arrangement, you might want to set out a few favorite things where your kids can reach them, and rotate them when they start looking for new things to explore. (This works for books too; one mom I know called it the Coffee Table Method of Homeschooling.) Indoors, throw a plastic tablecloth over the kitchen or dining room table and put a drop cloth on the floor. Or better yet, let the kids do their art and science projects outside.

The science and art portion of my home learning center is mainly housed in a large cabinet in the dining room. I've found that almost all the items in the cabinet do double duty for both subjects, so it makes sense to store them together. Many are recycled or repurposed or salvaged from old kits, toys, kitchen supplies, appliances, and so on. The rest come from hobby shops, teaching supply stores, and online retail sites. On the shelves I keep stacks of different kinds and sizes of paper, felt, craft foam, cardboard, and thin scraps of wood or metal, some of them collected into giant-sized ziptop bags. Different kinds of paintbrushes and ink pens are kept tip-up in oversized plastic cups. Below are drawers about as deep and wide as file drawers. In one, I line up fabric or vinyl book bags, each filled with all the materials needed for one specific craft project. In the other, I keep ziptop bags with bulkier items like egg

cartons, cardboard tubes, and bottle caps and jar lids, as well as leftover wrapping paper and gift bags. Almost everything else is sorted into clear plastic boxes, which are labeled and arranged on the shelves so I can find what I'm looking for with a minimum of searching. Here are some of the things they contain:

- Various kinds of beads; Popsicle sticks, toothpicks, and other wooden shapes; plastic straws in different sizes.
- Drawing and painting supplies, such as watercolor, tempera, and acrylic paints; pastels; markers; crayons; and colored pencils.
- Various types of modeling clay and similar materials, such as Play-Doh, bakable polymer clay, nondrying Plasticine, beeswax, and rolls of plaster gauze.
- Different kinds of tape (thin and wide clear tape, duct tape, electrical tape), glue (white, gel, super), and string, rope, and twine, etc.
- Tools that require supervision, such as hot glue guns, a heat shrink gun, an awl, and a small wire-bladed saw, are kept together in one box where I can keep an eye on them (especially important when working with a large group of kids).
- Magnets ranging from recycled business cards to horseshoe-shaped school magnets to powerful rare earth magnets that

need to be used under supervision.

- Optical tools such as mirrors, prisms, magnifying glasses, colored lenses, refraction lenses, polarized lenses, 3D glasses. I include laser pointers and other kinds of light sources such as ultraviolet (black light) and neon bulbs to use with them.
- Electronics ranging from different kinds of batteries to (mostly reclaimed) small motors, wires, electrical tape, LED bulbs, and old LCD screens.
- Chemistry supplies like baking powder, citric acid, various kinds of salts, food coloring and corn starch, along with plastic pipettes, measuring spoons and cups, and small plastic cups, plates, and bowls for mixing. Small amounts of things like corn starch can be scooped into a ziptop bag (labeled!) and placed in the chemistry box. Bulkier packages, as well as anything too dangerous or messy for kids to use on their own, are stored in a lockable bathroom cabinet and brought out upon request when supervision is available.

The rest of our materials are stored as close to where they are used as possible. The globe is on top of the bookcase that holds all the history, geography, and social science books. The microscopes (standard classroom type and a digital model for taking video and still images) are on or under a small worktable in between the living room and dining room and near an electrical outlet. Musical instruments sit atop the piano. Near the living room couch is the bookshelf for browsing or reference as well as chests of drawers filled with board games and movies. A tall baker's shelf

near the sliding glass doors is where we put our hydroponic and potted plants and small critters for study. The one exception has been construction toys like Lego, which get put away at night in the boys' rooms, to keep them from taking over the living room. Because our house is so small, bulky yarns and fabrics live in my room with the sewing equipment, and my husband's building tools get stowed in a corner of the basement and pulled out as needed. But a few smaller scraps can be kept down in the art cabinet, and I've got a "kid's toolbox" with small screwdrivers, pliers, and hammers under the worktable for quick access.

One other important aspect of a good learning center is having room to show off the projects and discoveries your kids make. If space is at a premium, arrange the best samples from a rock or leaf collection in a basket or dish, or create an arrangement of small works of art with other knickknacks and souvenirs. Some tabletop science projects, such as crystal radios, may even be attractive enough to keep on display. Hang up stamp or trading card collections in frames on the wall. For bigger works of art or temporary masterpieces, like sidewalk chalk drawings, take photos and collect them in albums or scrapbooks.

Over the years my family has made good use of our learning center. The items I included are the things I believe are the basics. But your learning center can reflect your family's interests, tastes, and surroundings. Whatever you choose to include will make it easier and more rewarding for your kids as they learn about and explore their world.

LEARN TO PLAY ONE THOUSAND BLANK WHITE CARDS

Kids are naturally creative, but they don't always get a chance to stretch the limits of their imagination. In school, as educator Sir Ken Robinson has said in his popular TED Talk—bluntly titled "Schools Kill Creativity"—children are taught that there's only one correct answer, and it's in the back of the book (and don't look, because that's cheating). Even outside of school, kids spend almost all their free time taking part in activities like organized sports that involve following rules and directions imposed on them by adults. The game known as "One Thousand Blank White Cards" is different. Invented by college students in the 1990s, it's a fast-paced game that gets better the more inventive kids become. And the only rules and directions to follow are the ones the kids make up themselves.

Absurdity is the hallmark of the game. Cards are often funny but nonsensical: "Does a pig love you? +10 points." But creativity is only part of what kids can learn from the game. As they find out through trial and error which new cards add to the fun and which are duds, they'll learn that it's OK to take a chance on something new and untested. Hopefully, they'll also learn a little about cooperation and respect: while practical jokes and teasing can be part of the game, it only works as long as everyone is still having a good time. (My older son thought it was hilarious in one session when his younger brother was handed a card that told him to play the rest of the game from the basement; his brother, not so much.) But mostly, One Thousand Blank White Cards is a game your kids will enjoy because they can truly make it their own.

$$$

$5 or less

30–60 minutes

Age 10 and up

Easy

- Index cards, preferably unlined (only 50–100 are really needed)
- Pencil or pen for every player

STEP 1: Prepare a Deck of Cards

The prologue to the actual game involves making up new cards. Players each get five blank cards and a pencil to write or draw whatever they like. Cards can give a player an extra turn, award or take away points, make up new rules, or challenge one or more of the players to answer a question or complete an action. They can also just have a silly phrase or drawing, which may inspire another player to write a companion card on the same theme. Here are some samples from real games:

- Awesome card! +500 points.
- Sideways time!
- Sideways time is over. Eat a pickle for 50 points.
- 2 + 2 = 10 in Base 4.
- Paper guilt: 27 trees died to make this card. (I don't know if that's true, but lose 500 points anyway.)
- Show off your ninja moves for 100 points.

These are then mixed into the deck of blank cards, along with any leftover cards from previous games. The blank cards in the deck can be filled in by players during the game to help themselves or just to keep the game lively.

STEP 2: Play the Game

Players start with a hand of five cards, and the deck is placed in the middle of the table. Going around the table, players pick one card from their hand and place it on the table (this is called "playing a card"). Players can play a card on themselves to gain points, or play one against someone else to subtract points. If there are directions on the card, they can play them on another player or on the whole group. At the end of a turn, players take another card from the pile. If the card is still in effect, it stays on the table; if its action is complete, it goes in the discard pile.

Determining who wins is up to the players. In most versions, the game ends when the entire deck has been played, and the person with the most points wins (unless someone has created a card that changes that rule so that the person with the *least* points wins). The game can also keep going until someone picks (or creates) a card that declares "Game Over." My kids and their friends usually didn't bother keeping score; they just played until they'd had enough and were ready to do something else.

STEP 3: Epilogue

After the game, players go through the deck to save their favorite cards and take out any cards that didn't make the game more fun to play. The remaining cards, along with more blank cards, become the seed of the deck for the next round of play.

Why Geeks and Homeschooling Are Often a Good Match

Many educational choices are available in the United States today, including public schools, private schools, charter schools, magnet schools, online schools, co-ops, and homeschools. We have the power of choice, to choose what educational arrangement best fits for ourselves, our children, and our families.

Each year, more families are choosing to homeschool their children for a variety of reasons, such as religious preference, socialization, educational rigor, time and content flexibility, gifted and/or special education needs, and kids' personal interests.

Although any parent can homeschool, geeks are ideally suited for it. Consider these qualities:

- Curiosity
- Self-drive
- An eclectic set of knowledge
- Love of learning

Would you say those were generally qualities of a geek, or of a homeschooler? If you said both, you would be right. Homeschooling almost seems custom-made for geeks. Most geeks tend to become experts in their interests, which requires time and flexibility—something that is usually missing in conventional schooling.

Homeschooling and the Geeky Parent

Many adult geeks today lead an autodidactic lifestyle in spite of, not usually because of, their particular educational experience. Imagine if the love of learning, and not rote memorization, were instilled from birth. As a geeky parent, homeschooling is ideal. You are put in the position of learning a variety of new things with your children. Also, your enthusiasm for favorite subjects comes through.

In the end, parents are the ones responsible for their kids' education, and by being enthusiastic about learning, geeks are well positioned to teach their own kids.

Homeschooling and Geeky Kids

Homeschooling provides an environment for self-directed learning. Because of this, once kids get to college age and beyond, they already possess the ability to seek out knowledge on their own.

A rigorous and complete education. Many schools have cut programs because of funding issues. They may have no electives, or no special services for the gifted or learning disabled. With homeschooling, you can tailor kids' education to fit their particular situation. If their passion is French poetry, they can spend extra time learning about it. If they develop an interest in particle physics, that interest can also be nurtured. Those kinds of choices in education rarely happen in any conventional setting.

Learning at their own speed. Some kids learn quickly, others take more time, and, for some, learning speed depends on the topic. Rather than go at the speed of the class average, you can teach your kids at the rate at which they learn, for example, if they need to study math at a slower speed, or work a few grades ahead of where they "should" be in reading comprehension.

Accommodating learning styles. Different kids best learn and retain information through different means. Some merely need to see something and they understand it. Some need to get their hands dirty and manipulate things. Most learn best when information is presented in a variety of ways. As a homeschooling parent, you can create the most effective learning environment.

Dig deeply into passions. If your kids develop a great interest in an obscure subject, or you want them to dig more deeply than normal into a conventional subject, do it! Between the internet and the library, free information is everywhere. Geeks often become very interested in one subject for a while and become immersed in it, and homeschooling allows for that opportunity.

A safe environment for learning. I would venture to say that, on average, geeks are more often ridiculed and bullied in school than the general population. Learning to the fullest requires feeling comfortable. With homeschooling, bullying can be eliminated, so kids are free to be themselves and learn in a nurturing, accepting

environment. Also, when your children are regularly shown that their opinions matter, it helps them grow up with self-esteem and self-confidence, and it doesn't squelch their creativity.

The World Is Your Classroom

Homeschooling can be an ideal geek lifestyle. Field trips can lead all over the country. Parents can take kids to museums during the day when they are actually open. Kids also see their parents doing normal grown-up things, such as grocery shopping, banking, and paying bills, so they get an accurate view of the daily life of grown-ups. Kids aren't sequestered all day with kids of the same age, but who likely don't have the same interests.

Homeschooling parents can involve their geeky kids with other geeky kids in the area. You can form science clubs, book clubs, or just play groups. The kids won't all necessarily be the same age, but dividing them up by age is pretty arbitrary anyway. Skill level and age don't always correspond. Interests and age are even less likely to correspond. Homeschooled kids will form friendships with kids and adults of all ages, which is much healthier than excluding anyone not in their age cohort.

Geek parents are often very well educated, with plenty of background knowledge for teaching. Their interests are usually quite varied, and it follows that geek kids' interests are, too. Once the basic subjects are covered (subjects that are required to be covered vary by state), you can cover any other subjects you deem important. Use your imagination. Some examples of more unusual topics to teach are geocaching, building siege engines, Lego design and construction, computer programming, robotics, traditional handicrafts, astronomy, formal logic, in-depth art history or music study, and foreign language at an early age.

One of the objects—or side effects, depending on your point of view—of homeschooling is to teach kids the value of independent, lifelong learning. As an adult, you teach yourself new things all the time. Most homeschooled kids learn how to do this much earlier than conventionally schooled children. When your children spend time exploring their own interests, sometimes by teaching themselves, they will be set for a lifetime of passionate discovery.

CARTOGRAPHY

making maps with kids

From drawing pictures or maps of their bedroom, neighborhood, or town, kids gain perspective on their surroundings. The world that our kids experience is different from our own. Theirs is slightly smaller, with the places they see every day taking precedence over their city, state, country, and the world. They also invent elaborate made-up worlds in their own imagination. Help your kids visualize and physically represent their real and make-believe worlds with this mapmaking activity.

$$$			
Almost free	30–60 minutes	Age 4 and up	Easy

materials

- Blank paper
- Colored pencils, markers, or crayons
- Blocks and figures (if making a model)
- Measuring tape and/or ruler (if drawing the map to scale)

STEP 1: Choose a Location

Considering the age and drawing experience of the kids involved, choose the subject for the map. For the youngest kids, their bedroom or the house would be a good subject. For older kids, a route to school or the town would be more appropriate.

STEP 2: Start Drawing

Ask kids to draw a map of the chosen location. For kids who may have fine motor skill difficulties, or for very young kids who don't yet draw well, employ the use of blocks, figures, and other toys to create a model of the area instead.

STEP 3: Get Creative

Kids need not restrict themselves to the world that they see, or even the real world. The maps they draw can instead depict the solar system, elaborate treasure or exploration maps, or even lands from their own imagination.

STEP 4: Expect Variation

The complexity with which kids draw maps increases as they get older. Most likely, younger kids will draw a front view of what they see, such as the front of a house. Older kids will draw an aerial view, including what would be seen from above. And kids in the middle will likely draw maps that include both front and aerial viewpoints.

Older kids can also practice drawing maps that are to scale. They can use a tape measure or ruler to measure real-life distances, and then shrink those by a factor of ten or more to represent the place on paper. The scale they use will depend on the size of the area they are representing.

If kids have no interest in representing the real world, allowing them to instead represent a fantasy world of their own design, or even one from a book (such as Neverland or the Land of Oz), will still give them plenty of practice turning a mental image into a map while keeping them interested in the project.

STEP 5: Broaden Your Horizons

Once kids have had practice drawing areas that are familiar, take a family trip somewhere like a ghost town, an amusement park, or a farm. After touring the location, have everyone (including you!) create a map for it. Then compare the results and find out what everyone noticed about the place.

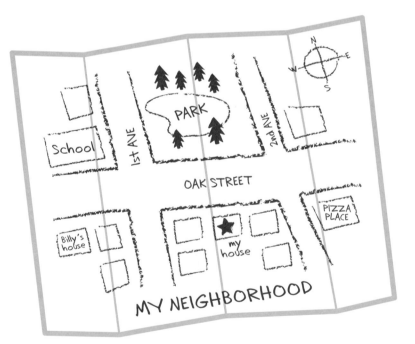

THE LOST ART OF READING MAPS

From giving directions to following a route on a map to understanding topographical lines, it is important for kids to learn to read conventional maps. Most of us grew up helping to navigate on road trips, or figuring out for ourselves how much farther it was to our destination, after driving our parents crazy asking, "Are we there yet?" for the umpteenth time.

Today's kids don't have the same experience we did. From GPSes in cars to Google maps that give turn-by-turn directions, most kids don't learn to navigate the old-fashioned way anymore. If they were lost in a city and all they had was a paper map, what would happen? What if they were out hiking and all they had was a topographical map and a compass? In either scenario, could they find their way to their destination?

To help your kids learn these valuable and potentially lifesaving skills, give them plenty of opportunity to practice paper map reading. Take your kids to a different city, or a new part of your own city, give them a map, and have them guide you somewhere. On your next road trip, show them where you are going and have them tell you where to turn. When you go for a hike, give them the trail map and have them lead the way. Or better yet, find a local orienteering club and experience the course together! Wrong turns will be a part of the learning process, but you will enjoy watching your kids figure it all out. Just be sure to bring extra water and snacks!

Fun with Words

Playing around with words is a clever way to sneak education into playtime. With very few or no supplies, you can spend hours with your kids, friends, or family exercising your word skills. Regardless of your age or ability level, word games can be a fun way to pass the time, to learn some new vocabulary, and to test your knowledge.

You can do anything your imagination dictates with words, of course, but here are several fun and challenging ideas for when Hangman and the Alphabet Game have worn out their welcome.

Group Storytelling. Storytelling is a great activity for two or more people. If you need ideas for stories, there are plenty of story starter websites online. If you'd like something more portable, check out products such as Rory's Story Cubes, a set of dice with inspiring images, or Once Upon a Time, a storytelling card game. Your group can each take turns telling a story, or each person can tell a small part of the story, moving around the circle to create an interesting and intricate tale. Storytelling is a fantastic activity for nuclear families, groups of kids, family reunions, or even for taking a break at work.

Word of the Day. Using a book, a calendar, or website (such as WordSmith .org or Merriam-Webster.com), find an age-appropriate but challenging word each day to teach your kids. Then try to work that word into conversation during the day as many times as possible. Perhaps try to work the entire week's worth of words into a story.

Crossword Games. Using a letter tile game like Bananagrams, create words or crossword patterns. Do it individually, or play as a group with a communal pot of letters. See if you can create a crossword pattern using all the letters in the pot, or have a challenge to create the longest word.

Create-a-Word Games. More conventional games, such as Boggle with cubes, Scrabble with tiles, or Quiddler with cards, give you the opportunity to create words out of a jumble of letters. This arranging and rearranging of letters is great practice for seeing the many possibilities in a puzzle.

Word Games for the Car. Word games are perfect to keep passengers entertained, and they are mentally challenging. These games require no materials.

- Pick a letter and list as many words as you can that start with that letter.
- Pick a category, such as food or animals. One person says a word in that category. The next person says a word that fits the category but starts with the last letter of the previous word. Keep going until you run out of ideas.
- Pick a topic and then, as a group, list things starting with all the letters of

the alphabet, from A to Z. Countries, cheeses, plants, or animals are topic examples.

- Each person takes turns thinking of a topic or concept and then describes it, but without using any of the words in the concept, like in the game Taboo.
- Pick a word, and then take turns saying as many words as you can that rhyme with it.

One, Two, Three. This game is for two players. Each person individually thinks of a word or phrase. Count to three together, and then each of you says your word at the same time. As quickly as possible, each of you think of another word or phrase that relates to both of the words you just said. Whoever thinks of their word first says, "One!" The second person to do so says, "Two!" Then you say, "Three!" together and say your new words. The game continues until you both say the same word at the same time. This game is cooperative, with the goal being to say the same word as quickly as possible.

THE ONE-LINE HORROR STORY

harness the power of a few carefully chosen words

Although it took me years to be able to admit this in public, I'm a big Stephen King fan. And thanks to the audio version of King's short story collections, which has helped us get through long car trips, my kids and I are now expert Stephen King critics. We'll stop a story in the middle to launch a heated discussion about how the plot line reminds us of another one of his tales, or to pick at the little quirks in King's writing that drive us nuts. (For me, it's the slang expressions he never gets quite right.) Horror stories have conventions that are easy to play with—or play off of. They are guaranteed to be thrilling and fast-paced. And they can also be very funny. Perfect for my family's literary taste.

So when it comes to encouraging my kids to write, the horror genre has usually been a winner. I suspect it's because of another attribute of horror stories—nobody takes them very seriously. As a writer and an editor, it's hard for me to resist the urge to start critiquing anything I read. But too much feedback and analysis can turn kids right off the process. So when we sit down to write stories, the only thing I look for is how much I enjoy the tale. By making a game of writing horror stories, I still give my kids the experience of planning out and producing a written work, but without any of the pressure of more "schoolish" types of writing assignments.

One exercise my kids and I enjoy is the very, very short story. For kids who are just easing into writing, it lets them compose an entire story in one burst of inspiration. It also lessens the chance they'll fall into the common trap of starting strong and then losing their way in the middle. They can write, read (or listen to), and—if they want—discuss their story in one sitting, so they get the instant gratification of seeing someone else's reaction to their words. At the same time, writing short-short-short stories focuses on some useful skills kids can use in any type of writing. For one thing, they'll find out how important it is to choose just the right word. And according to author Robert Swartwood, who coined the phrase "Hint Fiction" to mean a story that is twenty-five words or less, they'll learn the difference between random thoughts and a story that feels whole. But most important, writing fun little snips of microfiction leaves kids wanting more!

Perversely, when I stopped trying to teach my kids how to write, they got a lot better at it. Once writing became a pleasure instead of a chore, they began to come up with their own writing projects, alone and with their friends. Just the process of letting their ideas pour out and then reading them back seems to have taught them how to shape an effective piece of writing. Getting a reaction from their peers and collaborators has, no doubt, been helpful too. With their growing confidence and ability, my kids have even started to seek out their own mentors and guides, whether through workshops for teens or in books about writing by their favorite wordsmiths. (I like to think that listening to King read his own book *On Writing: A Memoir of the Craft* helped steer them in that direction!)

If you'd like to try short-short stories, it's simple to get started. You may actually find that it's easier to begin with a longer short-short—say, six hundred words—and then whittle it down as your kids gain experience. If you and your kids want to record their stories on audio or video, you can also set a limit on how long they take to read out loud; my kids' first attempt at microfiction was inspired by an NPR contest to write a ghost story that could be read on the air in three minutes or less.

If the storytellers in your house need a little help coming up with ideas to write about, here are some tried and true techniques:

Story starters. Also called "writing prompts," a story starter is any short sentence that stirs the imagination. The NPR challenge we tried at home for fun was to write a tale that began "Some people swore that the house was haunted," and ended with "Nothing was ever the same again after that." If you're really stuck, you can find examples on the internet.

Ripped from the headlines. I had a creative writing teacher in college who liked to have us come up with stories based on articles she cut out of the newspaper. One real-life idea I passed along to my kids was about an abandoned and crumbling insane asylum in New England that was being turned into luxury housing.

Do a takeoff of a familiar tale. For a longer short-short piece, one of my sons started with the standard "heir-to-a-fortune-must-spend-the-night-in-a-haunted-house" scenario, and then gave it a great comic twist. Suggest your kids take a scary story they know and make it funny, or a funny story and make it scary. What if instead of stumbling into the house of the Three Bears, Goldilocks sampled the breakfast bowls of the Three Zombies?

And just in case you don't believe that anyone can write a truly frightening story in twenty-five words or less, here's an example of a one-line horror story written by one of my sons when he was fifteen years old:

Problem Solved

The giant bugs were quelled by the giant bats. This was not an improvement.

Time Travel Through History

Picture this. You and your family would like to learn more about a time period from the past, but you would like it to come alive for everyone. Here is what you can do to "visit" history! Through the use of unit studies, which use a variety of school subjects to teach a topic in depth, the entire family can experience a piece of history together. Pick a time and place from history that the kids are learning in school, or choose one of personal interest to someone in the group. Then start planning.

Decide how many different aspects you want to include in your study. You can choose from such topics as clothing, food, games and leisure, music, art, literature, foreign language or vocabulary, government, history, science, math, maps and geography, important events, prominent men and women, and others. Then research the time and place and gather information and any supplies you might need.

If this is an activity in which your family will participate several times, it is also a good idea to create a history timeline and mark on it the events, people, and other details that you learn. Also take photos of any food or costumes you make, and include those on the timeline, such as your daughter wearing a ball gown or your son eating maize.

Any time and place in history will do, but strike a balance between broad and narrow topics. For example, the following choices are specific enough to focus your study but still leave enough room for you to have activity options: the colonial period in the United States of America, England during World

War II, Ancient Egypt, or the Industrial Revolution. Each time period you choose may offer a different set of topics to study, but getting information and activities for at least three or four of them will give everyone a good taste of that time in history.

I've put together a sample list for studying the U.S. Civil War. You need not study this many things in your unit study, but choose a few of them to start with. Then find clothing, books, recipes, songs, maps, and so on, to use on your activity day.

- *Clothing:* Uniforms of the Union and Confederate troops; women's fashions of the day including hoop skirts, corsets, petticoats, crinolines, chemises, slippers, bodices and skirts, parasols, bonnets, and fans.
- *Food:* Soldier rations such as hardtack, salt pork, condensed milk, peanuts, and coffee; gingerbread.
- *Games and Leisure:* Clay marbles, toy soldiers, blocks, jacks, trains, chess, checkers (known as "draughts"), backgammon, cloth or cornhusk dolls,

croquet, Charades, Twenty Questions, Blind Man's Bluff, Hide and Go Seek, and Duck, Duck, Goose.

- **Music:** "Farmer in the Dell," "Ring a Ring o' Roses," "Pop Goes the Weasel," "When Johnny Comes Marching Home," "The Battle Hymn of the Republic," "Camptown Races," "Dixie," and "Oh! Susanna," plus instruments such as the harmonica, jaw harp, drums, whistles, horns, and cymbals.
- **Art:** Mathew Brady's photography, Alfred Waud's sketches.
- **Literature:** Diaries and letters of soldiers, issues of *Harper's Weekly,* Sarah Morgan Dawson's *A Confederate Girl's Diary,* Mary Boykin Chesnut's *A Diary from Dixie,* slave narratives such as Harriet Jacobs's *Incidents in the Life of a Slave Girl* and Frederick Douglass's *Narrative of the Life of Frederick Douglass, an American Slave,* and the works of authors such as Walt Whitman and Emily Dickinson.
- **Vocabulary:** Antebellum, artillery, bayonet, bivouac, canteen, cavalry, Confederacy, Emancipation, infantry, kepi, knapsack, litter, Mason-Dixon Line, musket, muzzle-loading, secession, slavery, and Union, among others.
- **Government:** State secession, establishment of the Confederate States of America, and Reconstruction.
- **History:** Reasons for the war, including slavery, states' rights, economic and social differences between the North and the South, and the election of Abraham Lincoln.

- **Science:** Field medicine including amputations, anesthesia, chloroform, dysentery, morphine, scalpel use, tourniquets, and typhoid fever; the use of submarines; the use of the telegraph; the use of railroads in wartime; the Gatling gun; and ironclad warships.
- **Maps and Geography:** Maps of the United States before the war and after secession, maps of new states formed during the time (e.g., West Virginia), battle maps from major battles.
- **Important Events:** Major battles of the Civil War such as both Battles of Bull Run, Shiloh, the March on Atlanta, Gettysburg, and Antietam; the surrender at Appomattox Courthouse; the assassination of President Lincoln; the Gettysburg Address; and the Emancipation Proclamation.

- Prominent Men and Women: President Abraham Lincoln, Robert E. Lee, Ulysses S. Grant, Jefferson Davis, Dred Scott, John Brown, Harriet Tubman, John Wilkes Booth, Clara Barton, Thomas "Stonewall" Jackson, George McClellan, William T. Sherman, J.E.B. Stuart, and others.

The beauty of unit studies activities is that they can be tailored to any time period or place that interests you and your family. A bit of research ahead of time and some preparation is all it takes to spend an afternoon or an entire weekend immersed in another time or another culture.

WHERE ARE YOUR ROOTS?

Researching your family history and genealogy can be a very geeky pursuit. By its very nature, your tree of ancestors is never-ending, so there will always be more research to do, mysteries to solve, puzzles to figure out, investigations to pursue, and facts and figures to ponder. And whether you go back two generations or twenty, you will learn interesting facts about your history.

Along with learning about your ancestors, where they lived, what professions they held, and what social status they had, you will also learn about the history of the regions and places in which they lived. Perhaps you had an ancestor who fought in a war. Or suffered in the 1918 flu epidemic. Or came to the United States during a wave of immigration. Through your ancestor's personal and family stories, you learn about history from the perspective of real people, people to whom you are related. It puts a personal face on the past, which is the best and most interesting way to learn about it.

If many of your family members are from another country, researching your genealogy can also give you a good excuse to travel the world and see where your roots lie. Or your roots might be more conveniently located, just a few states away.

We are very lucky today to have the internet at our disposal. Genealogy research used to require more time-intensive work: writing letters, making phone calls, and undertaking trips to cemeteries and historical societies. That kind of legwork is still helpful, and in some cases is still the only way to get some information, but today most things can be discovered on the web. Through sites such as Ancestry.com and FamilySearch.org, and even through perusing some Google Books, you can search resources such as census records, military rolls, and published family history books. Searchable and cross-referenced resources make discovering relevant sources a breeze. It's an information addict's delight. You can also easily collaborate with others who are researching the same family lines as you, and you can even discover distant relatives who are currently living. If you really get stuck, you can hire professional genealogists to help you unearth a lost connection.

So climb your family tree, even if you only explore a few branches, or climb a generation or two. Chances are you'll learn something new about your family, and perhaps yourself, and your children will have a more complete context of their origins.

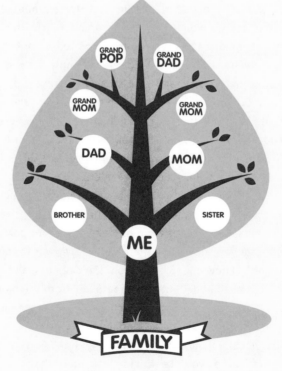

GRAND POP · GRAND DAD · GRAND MOM · GRAND MOM · DAD · MOM · BROTHER · SISTER · ME

FAMILY

COME AS YOU WERE PARTY

Want to show off what you know about your favorite period in history? Looking for a quick way to pack a lot of different history topics into one fun afternoon? Try throwing a "Come as You Were" party! This idea is perfect for homeschool groups and classrooms, but you can also do it at home with your kids' friends. Even kids who don't like having to memorize names and dates can get excited when it comes to dressing up and acting like someone else for a day. My sons attended a Come as You Were party when they were about eight and five, and it was a blast!

The party itself can be as simple or elaborate as you like. And because it's a joint effort by all the guests, it's not as much work as it might sound. Each child (or family, if you all want to get involved) picks someone from a specific time or place. It can be someone famous like Julius Caesar, or just an ordinary midwestern pioneer girl. You can focus in on one region or epoch, but it's much more fun to leave the choice open to your guests' imaginations—just think of what might happen when the caveman and the ninja warrior face off in musical chairs.

Now, to make it a party, you'll need food, music, and decorations. Games or activities or hands-on projects will give your guests a chance to mingle and get to know one another (in the form of their assumed identities). And of course they'll all want to dress up! This is where everyone pitches in. Using nonfiction books, stories, websites, videos, field trips, and any other resources you like,

each guest has to gather information on the kinds of things their person ate, wore, and did for entertainment, and come up with a way to share it with the other guests. It also helps to find out things like what their person's family life was like, and what the historical character did for a living. The more each guest knows about the culture and environment of the person they're going to represent, the more fun they'll have when it's time to meet up with other historical travelers.

To set up the Come as You Were party, you'll need room for the food your guests will be bringing. At our party we had dried venison from the Civil War Union soldier, cornbread from the pioneers, and Japanese rice and vegetables from the ninja. My own medieval knights brought grape juice in plastic wine goblets that we decorated with gold paint and glue-on jewels. And the Neanderthal (wearing little more than briefs and a large piece of fur slung over his shoulder) brought nuts and berries laid out on flat stones.

For entertainment, invite your guests to play and sing traditional songs or bring recordings of the music from their era. Some can probably teach a game from their time and place, or show how to make a simple skill or craft. If you want to give the kids a chance to present what they learned, you can let each bring an item for a show and tell, or they can take turns interviewing one another. (In a classroom or homeschool group, set up an area for the participants to display any books or other resources they used and other related projects they may have done.) But it's also fun to have your guests play modern-day icebreakers like Twister or Twenty Questions—keeping in character as much as they can.

So, with food, entertainment, games, and dress-up, a Come as You Were party is just as lively as a regular party. But does it help kids learn? Most definitely. Creating their own costumes, putting together their own dishes, and getting to play and act like someone else for a day—all with your help and encouragement—are the kind of focused activities that help cement information in the brain and create memories that will last a long, long time.

EXPLORING THE EVERYDAY WORLD AROUND US

It doesn't matter where you live, there's always something hidden in plain sight.

Once, when I was visiting my sister at college, we walked by a building that had a huge boulder in front. I asked her what the boulder was and she had no idea. It turned out the boulder was a way to signal the entrance to the geology department building. My sister had walked by it every day for the entire semester and never bothered to see what it was and why it was there. (She also graduated with high honors, obviously helped by her laser focus. My own college record is more scattershot.)

We see the world around us, but we don't always notice it.

The only thing you absolutely need to explore the world is an open mind. However, a pair of comfortable shoes helps a great deal. Other optional materials include a notepad, a camera of some sort for visuals, and an inquisitive child.

It makes no difference whether you live in a city or suburb or in the country. The first step to the world outside is noticing what's on the other side of your front door. Especially remember to look up. Often there are surprises when tilting the head toward the sky.

"It's a dangerous business, Frodo, going out your door. You step onto the road, and if you don't keep your feet, there's no knowing where you might be swept off to."

—*Bilbo Baggins, from J.R.R. Tolkien's* The Lord of the Rings

look for these things in cities:	**buildings**
	→ Similarities or differences in buildings built next to each other. It's usually clear which are the newer and older ones and that can provide clues to the shape of the original neighborhood. Or, conversely, show how intact it is, like the Beacon Hill area of Boston.
	→ Check for cornerstones. They'll provide the date the building was constructed. I used to pass an apartment building in Boston every day and became intrigued about its history. I checked the cornerstone date, looked it up, and found it used to be a school.
	→ Floor tiles, particularly in lobbies, are often unique, especially if the building is older. Even wooden floors sometimes contain hidden designs.
	→ Notice the shape and the type of the windows. Often, they've been modernized in older buildings but sometimes the original glass remains.
	→ Any regular occurrences either on a daily or weekly basis. This includes events as varied as bus routes, children leaving for school, and the line that forms at the coffee place at certain times of the day.
	parking lots
	→ A parking lot sounds boring. But taking note of the kind of cars, when the lot fills up, and when it becomes empty will tell a lot about the people who live or work in the neighborhood.
look for these things in the suburbs:	**patterns in the way the homes are placed**
	→ Either the neighborhood grew bit by bit or it came about all at once. The clues to the answer can be found in noting the style and lot size of the houses. In some cases, that's easy to see. With older homes, it's more subtle. On one street in a town where I lived, all the homes were little box houses built for people working in the local mill. Over the years, some of these have added garages, porches, second stories, and decks. But the design is the same underneath.
	any unique places, like the corner store or even the local greasy spoon or the playgrounds
	→ Even going behind parking lots can lead to unusual discoveries. In one small town, my son and I found fountains in a back parking lot. They were abandoned, in disrepair, and unconnected to plumbing, but each was about four feet tall. We had no idea why they were there, but their very presence was fascinating.

local paths between houses

→ Paths are cut between the rural streets where I live for better walking. One of them is along a pond that's losing ground to cattails and other plants and is slowly becoming a swamp. We have fun spotting ducks, geese, tadpoles, and other stuff, along with tracking how fast the shoreline is receding.

hiking trails at municipal or state parks

→ Not all are publicized or on maps. Sometimes it takes driving around to find one. My youngest son and I stumbled across a tiny state park on a back road in the town next to us last summer because I decided to try a new shortcut. The park had a mile-long walk around a large pond that was created as part of a short-lived canal system.

bike trails

→ These trails are often created from old railroad beds and that makes them great not only for biking but to see a little slice of the past.

a simple walk in the woods

→ Notice what kind of trees are growing and what kind of flora is on the ground. Try to guess where the little stream runs into a larger river. And leaf collecting is always fun.

When I was growing up in rural New England, I played in an area called the "cellar holes." I didn't think much of the name at all until I realized one day that the land had once been intended for development; holes were even dug for the foundations (the cellar holes) before the project was abandoned.

There are hidden elements everywhere, in any area of the country. The trick is keeping your eyes open enough to see them.

TOPOLOGY TRICKS

tic-tac-torus and möbius mazes

When I was a kid, I was fascinated by topology, the branch of geometry that deals with how shapes behave when they are twisted, curved, or stretched. Somehow—maybe it was the book *A Wrinkle in Time* by Madeleine L'Engle, in which the heroine, Meg Murry, travels across the universe by folding space—I found out about Möbius strips, Klein bottles, and other forms that exhibited weird properties or couldn't even exist in our three-dimensional world. Such advanced mathematical concepts are actually easier for children to grasp than adults, according to MacArthur "genius grant" winner Jeff Weeks. What's more, they can pique the interest of kids who never thought math was interesting before.

When my kids were younger, we got to meet Weeks and try out some of the games he developed as part of a NASA project to determine the shape of space. We were spellbound by his video of what space would be like if it were twisted like a Klein bottle and objects could be seen coming and going at the same time. As it turned out, data from the NASA probe seem to point to space actually being flat (or shaped like a twelve-sided die). But these topology tricks, adapted from Weeks's work, can still inspire budding mathematicians to reach for the stars.

I. TIC-TAC-TORUS

Free (you have everything at home)

15 minutes

Age 8 and up

Intermediate

materials
- Paper and graph paper
- Thin marker (for tic-tac-torus)
- Pencil with eraser
- Tape
- Copier (optional)

STEP 1: Make the Boards

Tic-tac-torus is just like regular tic-tac-toe—with one small difference. Instead of playing on a flat board, first you shape your piece of paper into a torus. A torus is a two-dimensional surface that is continuous in all directions. Picture a hollow donut. To make the donut shape out of a piece of paper, first roll it into a tube. Then curve it around so that the ends of the tube are joined. The tic-tac-torus board is joined only in one direction, to form a tube. But it has magical properties. You'll never have a tie game on it—there's always a winner!

To make the boards, first draw a few boxes about 4" (10cm) square on a piece of paper. Inside each box make a tic-tac-toe board, dividing each box into nine squares. (You can make copies of the paper if you want more boards.) Cut out each board around the outside of the border.

On the back of each board, attach a

length of tape along one edge so half of the tape is sticking out. Then roll the paper so the opposite edge overlaps the tape, and attach with the lines matching up.

STEP 2: Play

In regular tic-tac-toe, two players take turns putting an "X" or an "O" in the squares until one person gets three in a row. Do the same thing with your tic-tac-torus board. (It may help to stick your finger inside the paper tube to press against as you write.) On a torus-shaped board, you can just turn it and keep playing. Try it, it's amazing!

II. MÖBIUS MAZES

STEP 1: Prepare the Strip of Paper

A Möbius strip is a two-dimensional shape with one side and one edge. It's a torus with a twist! If you've never made one, cut a strip of graph paper the long way, about 1½" (3.8cm) wide. Flip one short end around, and tape it to the other short end. Voilà! Now, draw a line along the length of the loop; you'll go around twice before coming back to where you started. (To see something even cooler, try cutting one down the middle, then cut another one about a third of the way from the edge.)

To create your Möbius maze, draw while the paper is still flat. Cut a strip of paper as above and place it horizontally in front of you. Draw a border along the top and bottom edges (the long edges). On the short end on the left, start at the top and continue the border for about ½" (13mm). Leave an opening (one square wide on the graph paper) and then complete the border on that end. Mark that opening "A." Do the same on the other short end, except start at the bottom. Continue the border 1/2" (13mm), leave an opening, and then complete the border on that side. Mark that opening "B." In the center of the strip, draw a small star. This is your start/finish point. Draw a box around it, leaving two openings, each one square wide.

Now twist the strip to make a Möbius strip—but don't tape it yet. Where the edges meet, mark "A" and "B" on the blank side of the paper, making sure they match up with "A" and "B" on the side with the star.

STEP 1: MARK CENTER & EDGES

FINISHED FRONT

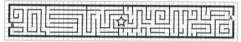

FINISHED BACK

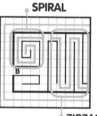

SPIRAL

ZIGZAG

STEP 2: Draw the Mazes

On your flat strip of paper, you'll be drawing three mazes:

- One to connect one opening of the star box with the star to point A.
- Another maze from the other opening to point B.
- On the other side, a third maze that goes from A to B.

To create a maze, draw a winding path one square wide from the beginning to the end. Leave openings along the way to add branches that will lead to dead ends. To make your maze harder to solve, use zigzags in your path and spirals for your dead ends. When you're done drawing, double-check that your paths still go all the way from beginning to end, and that all the branches lead to dead ends. If you have to, draw in pencil and use the eraser to fix any problems. When it's done, you can go over the pencil lines with pen, but make sure that the lines don't show through to the other side.

MATCHING UP "A" and "A"

STEP 3: Test Your Möbius Maze Puzzle!

Before you put your Möbius strip together, make some copies so you can share it with others. You will have to copy the front and the back separately, cut them out, and then tape them back-to-back. Make sure they line up the way the original strip does.

Now it's time to find some friends and see if they can figure out how to get through the maze from one opening of the box to the other.

FINDING MOZART IN METAL

rock me, amadeus

The inspiration for this activity comes from a curious place: an Iron-Maiden-obsessed ex-boyfriend. While listening to an album with him, I remarked how Wagnerian the music sounded, something I hadn't expected. I grew up listening to '60s rock, and heavy metal was about as far from my comfort zone as I could imagine.

My ex-boyfriend then made an offhanded comment about Bruce Dickinson, the lead singer of Iron Maiden, and his classical music influences. I was right, apparently. But the strange thing was, as I listened to the structure of the song I couldn't help but realize the truth of it. Just like in classical music, the songs often had themes that repeated throughout, changing and morphing, but always repeating. Not to mention the intervals and arpeggios.

I'm not the only one to make this connection. I later learned that there is an entire subgenre of metal called "symphonic metal" that fully embraces the connection.

Some kids take to classical music with no problem. For the most part my son enjoys it, though he clamors for rock and roll more these days. But I think it's important for him to know that most Western music springs from a single source, and that even the heaviest rock music uses classical music as an influence.

How do you make this applicable? Well, every kid is different. But here's some suggestions for bringing a fuller understanding of music history into your kids' lives.

Put a classical spin on your kid's favorite rock songs. A fun option for the musically inclined. Don't shy away from showy classical music either: Wagner and Beethoven and Bach have some pretty heavy pieces, after all.

Visit YouTube. Well, do it ahead of your kids, and search for various takes on the same songs. There are thousands of memes these days that show the crossover potential. One that comes to mind is the recent *Game of Thrones* theme music meme, where dozens of artists remixed it in different styles. My favorite is the heavy metal version; it's amazing how well it holds up.

Go beyond the classics. Another favorite crossover phenomenon is in bluegrass. Hayseed Dixie does AC/DC, but in bluegrass style, while the *Pickin' On* series does the same to classic rock acts like Led Zeppelin and the

Beatles, as well as more contemporary bands like Modest Mouse and singers like Sheryl Crow.

Go to the movies. If your kids are proving particularly classically resistant, you can't fail by starting with John Williams. If metal music or rock and roll doesn't inspire them, chances are you can reverse-engineer movie music.

Play them the Shire theme from *The Lord of the Rings* and then Dvorak's *American Suite*. Ask them what's similar and what's different; get them to pick out the themes and sing along with you. Maybe you'll end up with a four-piece harmony rendition of the theme from *Indiana Jones* while driving along to Grandma's next time!

FOR THE LOVE OF GEEKY INSTRUMENTS

Maybe it's that so many of us started off as band geeks. I don't know. But there is a definite fascination with musical instruments in the geek community. Acts like They Might Be Giants and Jonathan Coulton have pushed the limit of both classical and tech-based instruments, forever changing the landscape of nerd rock.

Here are ten geeky instruments we can't live without:

Accordion	*Turntables*
Ukulele	*Bagpipes*
Theremin	*Ocarina*
Keytar	*Lute*
Moog synthesizer	*Zendrum*

The Importance of Role Playing

 From childhood, we are programmed to role-play. We act out our fantasies in front of mirrors, playact with our friends, and imagine the most unlikely situations. It's an escape from the challenges of those early years, a way to balance our own hopes and dreams with what's actually possible. It's a way to never entirely let go of the impossible, I should say, while learning to be grounded in what is real and true. It's balance.

Then, for most people, it goes away. For some, too early. Whether it's at age ten or twelve or twenty, the majority of us stop pretending and get on with our lives. But there's no reason for it. In fact, I'd venture to say that it's downright dangerous for some kids, particularly geek kids, to lose a grasp on their imaginations at such a challenging time. I didn't have D&D as a kid, but I did have books, books I cherished so much I wanted to be a part of them. If it wasn't for Middle Earth, Prydain, and Narnia, I'm not sure what I'd have done with myself.

In particular, role-playing games like Dungeons & Dragons give kids the opportunity not only to use their imaginations, but to do so in a way that gives them control. This is a great contrast to the worlds they live in daily, the challenges at home and at school. Ethan Gilsdorf, author of *Fantasy Freaks and Gaming Geeks,* puts it best, reflecting on the importance of role-playing games in his youth:

Real life thus far had taught me that in the adult world, fate was chaotic and uncertain. Guidelines for success were arbitrary. But in the world of D&D, at least there was a rule book. We knew what we needed to roll to succeed or survive. The finer points of its rules and the possibility of predicting outcomes offered comfort. Make-believe as they were, the skirmishes and puzzle-solving endemic to D&D had immediate and palpable consequences. By role-playing, we were in control, and our characters—be they thieves, magic-users, paladins, or druids—wandered through places of danger, their destinies, ostensibly, within our grasp.

In spite of years of misunderstanding by the general public, role-playing games are seeing a tremendous resurgence. Conventions across the globe host adults and kids together, delving into underground caverns and laying siege upon castles. Gilsdorf goes on to explain that, while the naysayers have gotten a lot of press, role-playing games deserve a lot more credit than they're given:

D&D taught me vocabulary and verbal skills, math, statistics, and how to read maps; it developed my interest in history, flexed my imagination, and schooled me in team-building, personal expression, and interaction with others. I would always say, "Yes, I was a geek, but on balance, D&D was a good thing."

As parents, we can provide a safe, welcoming, wonderfully fun environment for our kids to dungeon-delve in, knowing that we're providing them so much more than a place to imagine.

Role-Playing Games for Beginners

I was late to the tabletop role-playing scene, and there are times I really wonder what it would have been like if I'd managed to join that D&D club in middle school. I mean, Dungeons & Dragons sounded so cool, even if I really had no idea what it was. Now I have the option to get my kids involved early so they'll never have to wonder.

My geek husband introduced me to tabletop RPGs not long after we started dating, when I was in my early twenties, and I really haven't looked back since. Some of the most enjoyable experiences I've had with friends in the last five years have involved us clustered around the dining room table, clutching our bags of dice, fighting monsters, making each other laugh to the point of crying, and telling fantastic stories.

It didn't take long for me to realize how awesome it would be to share that with my son, especially considering the width and breadth of possibilities out there (RPGs are no longer strictly for the sword and sorcery set). I think we gave him his first set of dice around the age of two. But that doesn't mean that bringing him into the fold has been easy, or without a challenge. The first rule of applying your geeky pursuits to your children is to remember that they will change all the rules.

The Setup

The heart of any good tabletop RPG is storytelling, and in my experience there's no age too young to start.

Set the scene early. Even my fantasy-resistant child enjoys a good dragon story now and again. Getting kids comfortable with the mythos of various realms isn't just good for future games, it's also great for their mythological lexicon. So many RPGs draw on mythology and folklore, it's also a history lesson in and of itself.

Learn to compromise. Our son didn't get excited about "nightly D&D" (i.e., D&D storytime) until my husband started adding car characters into it. Sure, cars aren't exactly canon. But they were a gateway into the setting, and that's certainly helped.

Go slow with the mechanics. Yes, we all dream of our sons and daughters rolling critical hits. But there's a lot of mechanics in the game, and if you rush it, they'll be overwhelmed. Get them familiar with rolling dice first, and doing simple arithmetic. That way they'll have a firm foundation to build upon when they do start.

The First Encounter

Few kids are ready to dive into the fight (especially the younger crowd). Throwing the rule book at your kid is likely going to end in heartbreak.

Start one-on-one. The gamemaster/player relationship is a challenging one, even for adults. So it's important that you understand your child's playing style and help him or her work out the kinks before you end up in a large group with potential disaster.

Start small. Work on the basic concepts of fighting, hit points, and so on, and try to naturally work them into the story. Throw away the manuals and charts for a while and simplify combat and hit points to the most basic components.

Don't be a control freak. Let your kid guide the story every now and then, and don't necessarily worry about the "fairness" of the game. Remember, your child is the hero. If you find that all he or she wants to do is control the game, well, maybe you have a budding Dungeon Master on your hands.

The First Campaign

Every kid is different, and it's up to every parent to gauge their kids' ability to play full-fledged tabletop role-playing games. But here are some good stepping-stones to help you get there.

Visit your local game store. When you feel like it's time for your kid to start playing a full-on campaign, resist the urge to go straight for the classics (unless you really feel like you're ready for that). In the last few years, tabletop RPGs have seen a revival, and there are dozens of great titles for every age. Utilize your friendly game store employee, crowdsource on Twitter. It might not involve mazes or monsters, but there's some truly imaginative, absolutely fun stuff out there that's a step along the way.

Plan small. You're not going to save the world in one campaign, not with kids. Nor are you likely going to have a game that lasts three to six hours. Set small, realistic goals (for you and your kid).

Invite others into the fold. If your kids are amenable, start a biweekly group after school. Remember, tabletop gaming is a social endeavor. It's about telling stories as a team and working together to solve problems. As a parent, you can't ask for a better tool!

Have fun! If things start getting too tense, remember: you are the parent. Dial it down a notch. Do a silly encounter with gummy worms. Play some goofy music. It's about connecting, not competing.

Suggested games and books:

- Heroica games by Lego
- *rpgKids* by Enrique Bertran
- *Happy Birthday, Robot!* and *Do: Pilgrims of the Flying Temple* by Daniel Solis
- *Mouse Guard Roleplaying Game* by Luke Crane and David Petersen

Nongeek Engagement

(just for mom)

Venturing Out into the Wild

The one thing I hear the most when people discover *GeekMom* is "I'm so glad there are other moms like me!" I completely understand. Growing up geek was hard, but being a Geek Mom can be even harder. Why? Society. Expectations. Social cues. These are all very difficult to navigate for some geek-leaning moms.

But what's important to remember is that it's not about what makes us different (our clothes, interests, and purses, to start) but what brings us together. I have a belief that more and more, moms are becoming geekier, mostly because of the role of technology in our lives. Even in the deepest, darkest jungles of suburbia, moms are turning to iPhones and online communities like never before. So while the thought of hanging out with your kid's new best friend's parents might give you hives: take heart! There is hope.

So here's one scenario (one that I've actually been in). You're at your local bookstore, in the children's section, and your child is otherwise engaged with another kid. The kid's mother is standing across from you, and she immediately strikes you as a nongeek. Not that it's possible she isn't one, but there are some hallmarks: Banana Republic outfit, designer purse, matching sneakers, and perfectly coiffed, highlighted hair. It's not just the visual cues. You immediately feel like you've been transported to ninth grade again, and you're in the presence of one of the Cool Kids.

You make eye contact and try to smile, feeling a little frumpy in your braids, faded TMBG T-shirt, and Etsy-purchased owl purse.

Here are some tips to get you through the next few minutes:

Keep it kid-centric. You have kids in common. Kids, geeky or not, share lots of traits and chances are you've had similar experiences. I've had some great conversations about kids' obsessions, for example. One mom explained how she just didn't get *Star Wars*, and I gave her some good tips for watching.

Keep it conversational. We geeks like to get going on subjects we adore, but this can be off-putting. Like in the *Star Wars* example above. I didn't start quizzing her on the spelling of Kashyyyk. I just kept it light and friendly. I doubt I'll ever see her again, but at least I didn't leave a scary impression of a *Star Wars* fanatic, thereby encouraging her to ban *Star Wars* from their house!

Play in the shallow end of the pool. Is she using an iPhone? Is her kid obsessed with *Angry Birds*? You might know a lifesaving app or site that could be of real benefit. Sure, it might not be top-tier geekery. But it's better than talking about sales at the J. Crew outlet, right?

Don't assume. Looks are deceiving. It's one of the central themes of children's literature. You never know what geeky tendencies lie beneath the surface of your kid's playmate's mom. She might be the world's biggest Buffy fan, and you just might not know it.

Play nice. When in doubt, smile. As someone who's been cornered about "those wonderful *Twilight* books" because I'm a writer, and well, a woman, sometimes this can be hard. If it gets really out of hand, you can always play the bathroom card, or pretend to get a text on your phone and reach out to your Twitter friends for help.

CHAPTER 3
RESISTANCE IS FUTILE

Multitasking Mothers Are at the Forefront of the Digital Revolution

Technology to many people means computers, gaming consoles, or what's commonly termed "grown-up" toys for men.

But in many ways, the digital revolution is being driven by women who see technology not as a toy but as something to integrate into their daily lives. The very first successful electronic-only book publishers were founded by women, and the books were written by women. Long before Amazon came out with the Kindle, women had been reading e-books, searching for stories not always available at the local bookstore.

Even gaming consoles show the effect of this integration. The Wii was targeted to families, especially as it's easy for younger kids to use and learn. But it was women who grabbed onto the games that they could make part of their daily routine, such as

Wii Fit, which is currently the third-best-selling console game in history. Today, there's an entire online community, the Wii Mommies, centered around the idea of using gaming to become healthier.

Moms are also using technology to keep in touch with our children, to streamline tasks that make our lives easier, and to informally educate our children through the ever-expanding use of learning apps for Apple and Android devices.

Often technology is bashed as something intrusive on family life or some interloper that will destroy human bonds. It's seen as a battle of traditional versus technological. But what many of us have already realized is that it's not a battle at all, that technology can be a great ally, not an enemy.

How to Recognize Safe Online Communities for Children

 While geeks know that the computer contains limitless resources, they're also aware that there can be just as many dangers, especially for children. But in today's world, it's impossible to keep children away from technology. And soon, children become old enough to want more than simple games or videos. They're going to want to do what we all do, which is interact with others online. That's where the scary part comes in, especially with the stories out there about predators who target children. However, while parents should be aware of this rare but dangerous problem, it's far more likely parents will have to deal with the fallout of frustration, anger, or sadness from a bad experience in an online community.

But just as you can make children aware of the dangers online, you can use a variety of ways to increase the odds that their online social experience is a good one.

The different online community models each have their own safeguards and privacy issues. There are MMORPGs (massively multi-player online role-playing games), discussion forums, and social media platforms like Facebook and Twitter, and, of course, whatever new toy comes along as our tastes change.

Some basic elements make up a good online community, which parents can check before giving kids the go-ahead.

First, check whether the site is well moderated. In the case of MMORPGs, that means checking to see if there are any age restrictions or software restrictions that make the game a more controlled experience. For instance, in the game *Wizard 101,* an all-ages game, it is impossible for players to insult each other when they're speaking online. The software looks for certain words and doesn't allow those to go through. Similarly, in Disney's *Club Penguin,* which is all about allowing kids to interact, there are moderators to notice and tag insults made. Any player who uses certain words will be automatically banned. I know this because my kids decided to see what would get them banned—pushing boundaries as they do—and they quickly found out how fast a banning can happen. Online games also often have levels that aren't accessible for those under a certain age, though be aware, if you have sneaky kids, they can lie about their age and the systems don't usually double-check that information.

On forums, look for any age limits first to make sure it's all-ages friendly. Second, look for the rules that are posted to be certain that insults and flaming aren't allowed. Third, spend time in the forum making sure those rules are enforced by active and involved moderators.

My eldest daughter, now grown, is part of a team of moderators on a message board for a popular young adult series. Moderators make certain the discussion stays civil and on topic as well as keep the discussion fun and lively for everyone. Having multiple moderators is key because the team can work together, brainstorm any issues, and also prevent one another from becoming petty tyrants.

On most well-run boards, the posters themselves will check each other if someone steps over the line, sometimes even before a moderator can get involved. This is a sign of a strong community.

Social media platforms like Twitter, Facebook, and whatever successors develop in the coming years are full of potential problems for children. They're unmoderated, unfiltered, and allow basically anyone to talk to anybody at any time.

Children often have no notion of their own privacy so they have a tendency, even as teenagers, to put far too much information about themselves in public. This is changing a bit as today's teens recognize that even college admission departments are

double-checking their Facebook pages and other social media to learn about them. But rather than simply banning kids from going online, it's sometimes better to just make them aware of the pitfalls.

Let kids know that anything they post publicly stays public forever and ever. Make sure that if they set up a Facebook page or a blog, it's private and others can read by invitation only. And make sure they know there are literally millions and millions of people out there and while the vast majority are great, many can be hurtful, mean, and juvenile. This can be a teachable moment in that it's a chance to show children what behavior is acceptable and what behavior is over the line in social situations.

But younger children especially can get overwhelmed. Holding off on the unmoderated Wild West free-for-all that is open social media is a good idea until they've had a chance to try out online communities in a structured setting.

Why I Let My Kindergartner Play World of Warcraft

 I spent a good deal of time toward the end of my first pregnancy (and, indeed, in the years leading up to it) playing a gnome warlock named Ardelia in *World of Warcraft*, arguably the most well-known MMORPG in the world. The premise of the game is simple. You go on quests. You get stuff. You go on more quests. You get better stuff. Along the way you discover an amazing world full of mythical creatures and races, steeped in its own mythology and teeming with monsters, challenges, and dungeons. And all this is made much, much better by playing with friends and, in my case, family (my sister and brother-in-law).

I'm a bit of a fantasy geek, and while I was late to RPGs of both the tabletop and online varieties, for the majority of my twenties, fun likely meant raiding a dungeon or spending the evening questing and raiding with my husband, Michael, and our guild.

When our son, Liam, was born, we all but stopped most of this sort of activity. I mean, who really has time with a squalling newborn and essentially no sleep at all? Okay, so maybe some people manage it, but we certainly didn't. It wasn't until Liam was around two that we really started to get back into the game. And that's when he discovered it, too.

My first inclination was to prevent him from playing. It's not as if *World of Warcraft* has much in the way of blood, but there's a good amount of violence: lots of slaying monsters, from kobolds to dragons. I worried what exposure to constant death, however cartoonish, might do to him. What could he gain from playing at this age?

But my husband gave me puppy eyes. We'd dreamed of this day, and now here our son was practically begging for entrance into Azeroth. Well, I conceded, on the grounds that Michael was going to play along with him, and if there was any chance our son was scared or uncomfortable, we'd shut it off and find something more age appropriate (video games are an inevitability in our house, after all, between his mom's obsession with *Dragon Age* and his dad's enthusiasm for everything else).

It turns out, my worries were completely unfounded. Not only did our son not want to quest, he wasn't even particularly interested in the slaying of creatures. Nope, he wanted to fly on the gryphon, high above Azeroth, for as long as possible. It wasn't about death and destruction, it was about exploration. It was about seeing the world drop away and beholding unexplored vistas and landscapes. I will never forget watching him, perched on my husband's lap, squealing with delight over each mountain range and castle emerging from the horizon.

Clearly, it was the journey, not the destination.

As we say many times in this book, much of parenting comes down to simply knowing what your child is capable of and prepared for. In many cases, there's no tried and true way to tell if your kid is ready for RPGs, let alone any video game. Obviously, now at five, our son is still years away from entering unchaperoned. But he's taught us, above all, that even though we may think we know him, there's always room for surprise. Seeing Azeroth through our son's eyes taught us more than I think he'll ever realize.

SIMPLE WEBSITES FOR CHILDREN

I call my youngest son the tech genius minion because he's been mad for the computer since he first could peck at the keyboard. He taught himself to read using browser instructions such as "stop," "go," "forward," and "back." But as he grew older, he wanted to create his own stuff for the computer. Specifically, he wanted to create his own website.

I stood back and out of his way while, at age ten, he gathered up all sorts of HTML, JavaScript, and website-building books and built his website. But there's a much simpler and no-cost way to start from scratch that even the most tech ignorant can do.

STEP 1: Plan the Site

The very first element of a good website requires no technical knowledge. It requires knowing what you want to present. A website should have a reason to exist.

For example, if your child is creating videos and wants to publicize his or her YouTube channel, that's an excellent purpose for a website. It should contain the three basic elements of all good websites: the landing page, an about section, and an archive of all works. Using our example of publicizing a YouTube channel, the landing page could have a banner image, a header describing the purpose of the site, and the latest video creation. The "about" page would have an explanation of who's behind the videos and production

and cast credits. The archive page would have links to the overall YouTube channel and some of the most popular videos.

As with anything, it's much easier to create a website if there's a plan.

STEP 2: Use Already Created Templates

After the plan, then it's time to go looking for website templates. One of the easiest places to create a website is weebly.com. It has simple instruction at the top of the page via tabs, everything to add pages is click and drag, and if the child becomes proficient, upgrades are available to allow customization. Creating two pages and some text on weebly.com took me all of five minutes. I suspect it would take longer for someone completely new to website building, but everything is intuitive, and trial and error is a great teacher, especially as nothing is public until the "publish" button is pressed. The downside, however, is that once the basic weebly site is mastered, it costs to upgrade and add features, such as videos.

Free

Varies

Any child who is reading
can attempt it

Easy to difficult,
depending on method

materials
• A computer and a wireless connection

special skills needed
A base understanding of what goes into websites

WordPress is less intuitive but has more free features. It's easy to sign up for at Wordpress.org and that will take you to a dashboard that seems to be, well, gobbledygook for the nontech person. But there's a method to the madness.

First, choose a theme or a "look." WordPress, like weebly, will present a number of choices. Posts can be added via the "add new" post button. The next important element is "pages," which will put several little tabs on the top of the site so anyone visiting could click on "latest blog post," "about," or "books by the author." There is a nice menu at the top of each post that allows posters to upload photos or videos, change fonts, insert links to other places, and generally make the post look professional. Make sure the child masters all the buttons at the top of a blank post first before letting them move on to other stuff, such as inserting widgets. Those are fun but for the advanced.

STEP 3: Creating from Scratch
Starting with a blank slate is the most complicated way to create a website and there are a plethora of books that teach how

to do it. I won't try to duplicate that teaching in such a short space, especially since the technical elements may change over time. But, briefly, there are three elements to creating a website from a blank slate: technical codes to put up images and text, a free web host, and knowledge of how to upload the coded files to your website.

The first thing to do is find some good, recent HTML-coding tutorial sites, like lissaexplains.com or w3schools.com. They will teach the basics of how to convert images

and text to a computer language that will create your site.

The next step is to put the website coding together in a free program like Notepad++.

Free web hosting can be found with a site like free-webhost.com. The uploading of the files to the website pages is done via a file transfer protocol, or FTP. One such program (an FTP client) is FileZilla. Many tutorials on how to use this program and others like it are available on the web.

While this route is more complicated and it will take the most time, effort, and patience, it's also the most flexible.

Being Online Before It Was Cool

 In the days before the internet was available to the public, BBSing took the place of IRC, e-mail, and forums. There were no safeguards in place, but from teens up to adults, BBSes (Bulletin Board Systems) were online hangouts that often replaced in-person social lives.

BBSes ran on computers with programs that allowed people to connect to them with a modem. A variety of programs were available to use, each one customizable by the sysop, or system operator, who ran the BBS. The sysop set everything up, ran the BBS from his or her computer, and kept everyone in line. Sysops were usually nice and responsible, but a few were grumpy or unreliable. Most BBSes had just one phone line going into them, allowing only one person to connect at a time.

When I was about thirteen years old, my mom bought a computer, our first useful PC. It was an XT Clone with a top speed of 8 mHz in turbo mode and a 1200 baud modem. It had two 5¼-inch floppy disk drives, and we soon added a 10 MB hard drive. I wasn't sure what to do with the thing right away. It was novel, but I didn't use it for more than word processing for school. That is, until one of my best friends introduced me to BBSes. She told me that there, you could write messages to other people, participate in discussions, upload and download files, and, on those with multiple phone lines, chat in real time. She gave me phone numbers for a few decent local BBSes, and she helped me learn how to dial up.

Right away, I realized that I needed to

have an alias, a nonreal name to represent me in the online world. No one used their real name online in those days, and your alias was supposed to reflect your personality in some way. I struggled with choosing an alias, but was excited to get started, and finally just picked the first thing that came to mind. So my alias was "Peewee."

I started participating in BBS discussions and quickly made friends, but then learned that my choice of alias made the (almost entirely) male population on BBSes think that I was a boy. Once word got around that an actual girl was on the message boards, however, I made plenty more friends. Fortunately I was old enough and savvy enough to be wary. No one ever gave me any inappropriate attention. Perhaps I was lucky, but I tend to think that it was a "the (online) world was a safer place back then" kind of situation.

After a week of exploring this new-to-me world, I was hooked. At school I had always been the geek, the one to make fun of. I was very shy to begin with, and I was made even more shy because of how I was treated. But on BBSes, I was able to be myself.

I soon got involved with a couple of multi-line BBSes, where you could hang out in the chat room and talk to other people. This kind of chatting helped my typing speed improve quickly, and I began to learn to "speak" through my fingers, typing the patterns of words instead of individual letters. Also, I became much closer to many of my BBS friends by chatting.

BBSing took the place of most of my socializing during my high school years. After school, I would rush home and get online, catching up on what I had missed. I conversed with adults and other teens alike. I dated people I met online, back when that idea was scoffed at. But since the BBSes were all local, I could meet up with my online friends in person at BBS parties or other get-togethers. The events were often weird and awkward, but no one seemed to notice.

In retrospect, I can't believe that my mom let me have free rein to be online and meet friends in person. I'm sure there were some creepy people out there, but I never encountered one or heard about any.

Eventually, BBSes made way for the internet, first giving us access to things like Gopher, Archie, and Usenet, and then eventually developing graphical interfaces that made using the World Wide Web more user-friendly. Today's internet includes social media and the always-on smartphone to connect us all. The days of confused looks about being online are gone. Now being online is assumed. What used to be nerdy and foreign is now taken for granted. Though BBS history is still unknown to most people, these virtual bulletin boards helped pave the way for the internet we know today.

Before They Were Machines,

computers were people

The history of modern digital computers is relatively short, well documented, and easy to tell, but computers started out as people, not as the machines we know today. The word *computer* was coined in the early to mid 1640s. At the time, it didn't refer to a machine, but rather to a person who did computations. Let's go back in history and learn a bit about how things were done by hand, before digital, or even mechanical, computers were invented.

One of the earliest needs for computation, especially from 1700 to 1900, was for astronomical calculation. Astronomy was a prominent science of the time, and calculating the movement of heavenly bodies required quite a bit of number crunching. This was time-consuming for one person to do, so people often worked in teams. Computations were then broken down into steps, with each person working on one part. This was an early form of parallel processing. This division of labor made computation more efficient, since each computer could specialize in his or her own task. It also saved time by eliminating task switching.

One of the first cases of such mass computation involved the eighteenth-century passage of Halley's comet. Astronomers had predicted that the comet would arrive sometime during 1758, but French mathematician and astronomer Alexis-Claude Clairaut wanted to more accurately estimate the comet's arrival. Clairaut had two assistants to help with his computations, one of whom was a woman. The three computers used the masses of the sun, Saturn, and Jupiter to compute the arrival of the comet, since those bodies were large enough to alter the comet's path and thus affect its arrival date. The three friends all sat down at a table together, in the Palais Luxembourg, and worked through the problem, day after day, often working through meals. Each one would work on a slightly different part of the problem, and they eventually came up with an estimate of the comet's arrival. As it turned out, while the comet was spotted near the end of 1758, it didn't reach perihelion until 1759 (perihelion is the point in the comet's orbit where it is nearest the sun). The actual perihelion was only about one month before the estimated date, which at that time was quite within the acceptable error margin.

Dividing labor for computation was soon also applied to nautical navigation figures and almanacs. When the metric system was developed, it was also used by a team led by Gaspard Clair François Marie Riche de Prony, a civil engineer with France's Corps of Bridges and Highways. His team of ninety-six computers produced seven hundred calculations per day, working to create logarithm tables for metric angle measurements that, unfortunately, were never widely used.

Soon the idea of automation made computation more interesting. English mathematician Charles Babbage joined the Astronomical Society of London with his college friend John Herschel. In 1821, the two worked on one of the Society's first projects, mathematical tables that would be added to the British *Nautical Almanac.* They hired two computers to create the tables, and then compared the results. Since there were so many differences between the resulting numbers, Babbage considered that using a machine for this process would make the answers more accurate. He went on to invent the difference engine in 1822, which was a mechanical calculator designed to solve polynomial functions, and later the analytical engine, which was a programmable mechanical computer.

As time went on, travelers to North America brought these methods of computation with them, and once the Industrial Revolution and automation began in force, the United States pushed for more progress in science.

In Cambridge, Massachusetts, work started on creating an almanac for the United States. The people in charge tried to recruit some mathematicians as computers, including French astronomer Urbain-Jean-Joseph Le Verrier who, through pure calculation and not direct observation, discovered the planet Neptune. Though Le Verrier's fame would have helped the almanac project, he declined, along with almost all the mathematicians who had been contacted. Those in charge instead started looking for students, independent

astronomers, and skilled amateurs to do the work.

After the Civil War, more women were to be found in computing rooms. More doors are often open to women during and following wartime, including in government, and those women who were good at manipulating numbers often turned to computing instead of general clerical work. In fact, in 1880, the Harvard Observatory's computing staff was composed entirely of women. Part of the reason could be, though, that women were paid about half as much as men for the same computing work, so meager budgets might have only allowed for hiring women.

In the late 1800s, computers in the United States were college graduates. Many were from the new women's colleges, including places like Radcliffe and Bryn Mawr. There were computers in other parts of the world as well. A mathematician named Radhanath Sikdar was a computer for the Great Trigonometric Survey of India. He calculated the height of Mount Everest, showing everyone that it was the highest mountain in the world.

Halley's comet came around again in 1910, though by this point scientists knew that it was a recurring comet. There were no lingering astronomical questions that calculations would help solve this time around, so some felt that computations were unnecessary. Others disagreed, believing there was still usefulness in the work, if only to correct past computational mistakes.

By this point, computers used slide rules, calculating machines, math tables, and other resources for the task. Calculus and differential equations were also employed. Each time Halley's comet came around, the methods and

computations used became more and more accurate.

By the turn of the twentieth century, computers were being used in more fields than just astronomy. Other sciences such as meteorology, engineering, and statistics had their own computer rooms. During World War I, computers, many of them women, were used in army ballistics and other wartime efforts.

During the Great Depression, the Works Progress Administration (WPA) funded work for scientific programs, including a computational project to improve and expand existing mathematical tables. It was called the Mathematical Tables Project and included work on exponential numbers, the function ex, and more. Computers came from the many unemployed workers, most of whom were not well educated. As before, large problems were broken down into simpler steps, which in this case were addition, subtraction, single-digit multiplication, and long division. Workers were divided into four groups, each of which handled one of the steps. If they encountered anything that fell outside their group's task, they would hand the work off to another group.

Soon machines took over more and more of the work that was previously done by hand. At first, the machines weren't more efficient than a person, since they required a lot of setting up. Because of this, physicist Richard Feynman was still preparing computing plans for a group of human computers during World War II. Again, larger problems were broken up into addition, square roots, division, and so on. To put the humans and machines to the test, however, Feynman held a race between human computers and punch card machine computers to see which was faster. Though both sides were about even for a while, eventually the humans tired out, while the machines kept up their pace. Human computers were still faster for many things, though, since the machines required so much preparation. It wasn't until after the war that machines pulled ahead, and the age of the human computer came to an end. The last computer offices were closed during the late 1960s.

For the most recent return of Halley's comet in 1986, computations were still being done to calculate its arrival. This time, however, such calculations were done using a program written in FORTRAN IV instead of using paper and pencil. And as with each previous calculation for the comet, the discrepancy between calculated arrival and actual arrival shrank, this time to under six hours.

Computers, as we know them today, do a lot more than just calculations. We use them as a tool for everything from accessing the internet to playing games.

But computers were once people, calculating small parts of a larger problem, with speed and efficiency. These groups of workers, these computers, are often left out of the history books. They worked hard at the low end of things, not visible to most people. They didn't fight to make their stories heard, and now knowledge of them and what they accomplished is often lost to history.

For more information about this fascinating topic, please read *When Computers Were Human* by David Alan Grier. He goes into great depth about the role of human computers, and particularly the history of women in the profession. The book is very well researched and discusses a topic rarely covered elsewhere.

ADA LOVELACE: GEEK GODDESS

Name: Ada Lovelace **// Lived:** December 10, 1815–November 27, 1852 **//**
Occupation: Writer, Mathematician, Computer programmer, Mom **//**
Known for: Writing the first computer program

Born Augusta Ada Byron in London in 1815, living a hundred years before the development of the modern computer, Ada Lovelace is thought to have written the first computer program. She was the daughter of Lord Byron, but was raised by her mother, who especially encouraged her in mathematics.

Lovelace was often ill as a child, but she still kept up her education. One of her tutors introduced her to the mathematician Charles Babbage. She became interested in his work, including his mechanical difference engine. This engine was for working with polynomial functions, which could be used to calculate a wide variety of useful things. The difference engine inspired Babbage's mechanical analytical engine, which included additional features such as the ability to do arithmetic, conditional branching, and loops, and it also contained memory.

Ada married the Earl of Lovelace in 1835; they had three children, but that didn't keep her from working on her mathematical studies. Babbage asked Lovelace to translate a book describing his analytical engine. The notes and calculations she added are longer than the book itself, and included a process for how the engine could calculate "the Bernoulli numbers," a sequence of rational numbers recognized for their importance in mathematics, numerical analysis, number theory, and differential topology. If the engine had actually been built, her method would have worked.

This method is what many historians consider to have been the first computer program. Lovelace also saw many more uses for programming than even Babbage did, such as for composing music or making graphical representations. He gave Lovelace the nickname "the Enchantress of Numbers." In the end, he never fully built either of his engines, and Lovelace's health declined while she was still young. Her short life remains an inspiration to women and girls in math, science, and technology.

The Nintendo Generation Comes of Age

 There is a photograph in existence that documents the precise moment when video gaming became more than "just games" for me. It's Christmas 1989. My sister and I are in matching blue-and-white flannel pajamas, balancing a gift between us on our knees. My hair is cut in an embarrassing pageboy do, and my mouth is frozen in a look of shock and awe as my sister paws away at more wrapping paper. Beneath the holiday pattern you can read: "Nintendo . . ." and see the outline of the gray console and black background.

That's the moment everything changed.

As for millions of other kids in the '80s and '90s, the Nintendo became the center-piece of video-game entertainment at our house. Before, we'd had an Atari 2600 (upon which I'd cut my teeth, eventually beating *Galaga*). But it was the Nintendo that became a household obsession, shaped the language in which we spoke to our peers, laid the foundation for our geeky tendencies, and, ultimately, brought us all together.

We know their names. Princess Peach. Princess Zelda. Link. Donatello. Starfox. That damned dog in *Duck Hunt*. We know their catchphrases ("Your Princess is in another castle"), and we know their theme songs (just try humming the *Super Mario Bros.* theme song around me; I can't resist, I have to keep singing it). We know the obscurities (*California Games,* anyone?), and we know some will never be surpassed, even today (*R.B.I. Baseball*). We laid the groundwork for the billion-dollar franchises of today and still move the market.

As a girl gamer, I'm forever indebted to Nintendo. Why? For *Super Mario Bros. 2,* which, as off canon as it is, allowed me to play a female character for the first time. There's a lot of power in that, and I think video-game companies are still figuring that out. Women, by and large, have not been the target market for video games. The last ten years have seen that trend reversing, with predominantly RPG-style games allowing for complete character customization, regardless of gender. If it hadn't been for Princess Peach, though, I think I'd have been more reluctant to play. Sure, she was slow as hell. But she had a pretty pink dress, and for a pre–Disney princesses–obsessed girl like I was, this was a one-way ticket down the geeky path. I've never looked back.

What I love about the Nintendo generation is that we really haven't grown up. But we have jobs. And kids. We're mothers and teachers and bankers, lawyers and layabouts. And as different as we are, as many degrees of geek as there may be between us, we still have some golden years in common, and we still get excited seeing the newest Mario or Zelda incarnation.

It probably has to do with working in the games industry, but I love overhearing some of my coworkers talking about new games coming out. These guys are programmers and producers, people who are steeped in the business of games. But hearing them discuss *Skyrim* or whatever newest game is out always gets me smiling. In spite of being surrounded by games, they still love the stuff. They're übergeeks, for sure, but they haven't lost their childlike wonder when it comes to new games.

Sure, we may be hesitant to get into the Kinect, but that's part of coming of age. Embracing change is always difficult. Yet still we get thrilled for every new release, and, let's face it, we became nostalgic for 8-bit before we even hit our thirties. We might not have Woodstock or grunge or *Pretty in Pink.* But we'll always have video-game symphony orchestras and Princess Zelda (who looks good in pink or in blue).

Tech for Preschoolers
education versus distraction

 I'm shopping with my five-year-old son at a department store, and he's almost unhinged. Rather than stay near me, he's taking every chance to dart in and out of the clothes racks, roll around on the ground, and do everything possible to distract me from my task. I'm feeling frustrated, exhausted, and completely unable to focus. Then I hear a familiar sound: a bird flying through the air, colliding with a structure, and cue the music.

I peek over the rack and see another mother with her son, a few years younger than mine; the kid is plastered to his mom's iPhone playing *Angry Birds,* just like my son does when I let him. Part of me thinks she's smarter than me, that I should have just put my son in a cart (even if he may be over the weight limit) and let him play to his heart's content. Part of me is glad I had a policy that on outings, he doesn't get to play his games.

That's the challenge, these days. The saying used to go "born with a silver spoon in his mouth," but now it's more like "born with an iPhone in hand." Our son was born in 2006 and has never known a world without iPhones, touchpads, and computer screens. We have a video of him playing on our MacBook at three months old, giggling and spitting up (the horror . . . all over the keyboard) as the computer chimed in "baby mode" making shapes and sounds. We thought it was the cutest, geekiest thing in the world, and he was all smiles. Yes, at times, I'm remarkably thankful for these technologies. But sometimes I wonder: How much is too much?

I feel like my son's generation is going to be spoiled with technology no matter what I do. The truth is, eventually his technology will even outpace me. And my technology will seem obsolete to him (I found my husband's old Game Boy a few years ago and gave it to my son, who ruled it was unplayable because the screen didn't engage when he touched it with his finger). But right now, during his formative years, it's my responsibility as a parent to teach him to balance.

While my son loves *Angry Birds,* and we do let him play it on occasion, we've done our best to keep these sorts of simple games as rewards. Honestly, they're brain candy, at best teaching cause and effect and dubious physics. When it comes to educational games we try to keep as collaborative as possible. In preschool, they're just developing language and basic math skills, and it's most helpful if parents are involved as much as possible. We notice he tends to go inward with even learning-based games, and getting him out of it can be difficult.

Whatever games you choose, whether or not they be educational, any screen time should be limited. Countless studies have been conducted on the brains of young children, and while we may not have a definitive answer, I think it's safe to err on the side of caution. As tempting as it is—and yes, sometimes we have to use games as bribery or a technological pacifier—technology shouldn't be a Band-Aid or a coping mechanism. When it comes down to it, apps on the iPhone or Android can be great tools when used as part of their education, but they should never be the centerpiece. No matter how far technology goes, kids still need plenty of hands-on experience, plenty of fresh air, lots of social interaction, and present, loving parents.

Geek mom
APPROVED APPS
FOR PRESCHOOLERS

- Doodle Buddy
- Famigo Sandbox
- Monkey Preschool Lunchbox
- Dr. Seuss Band
- Don't Let the Pigeon Run This App
- Harold and the Purple Crayon
- A Monster at the End of This Book
- KinderApp
- LetterSchool
- NoodleWords
- Lego App4+
- Toca Robot Factory
- Toca Hair Salon
- Toca Tea Party
- Toca Doctor
- Slide-a-ma-jig/Mix-a-ma-jig
- Cars2 AppMates

FITNESS FOR GEEKS AND GAMERS

Running. Lifting weights. Aerobics classes. Exercise DVDs. Although these more traditional methods are still viable options for personal fitness, many of today's geeks, especially geeky moms, are turning to technology to make exercise fun and convenient.

With the advent of the Nintendo Wii and Wii Fit, game systems started being a viable option for exercise and fitness. Wii Fit's sudden popularity quickly spawned other fitness titles, by both Nintendo and other game publishers. Many people started turning to these games to get fit and lose weight, often with great success. Now there is a wide variety of titles to choose from, including games that focus on aerobics, strength, general fitness, and even dance. The dance games in particular get kids moving along with their parents.

In addition to game systems, other kinds of technology have played a significant role in adding more fun physical activity to our busy lives. For geeks who like data, data collectors like the Nike+ and its accompanying app have given runners plenty of numbers on which to ruminate. Other running devices integrate GPS, adding maps to the data-geek's dream.

There are also plenty of general exercise apps where you can set fitness goals and log exercise. Some apps instead focus on diet and food, helping you count calories

or look up nutritional information. And most of these health and fitness apps also have numbers, graphs, and charts to help you closely monitor your progress.

Not to be outdone, other websites will help you reach your diet and fitness goals as well. The Weight Watchers website allows you

HI SCORE:
314,159

to keep track of your food and exercise and gives you plenty of data in return. It is a great option for losing weight if you don't live near a weekly meeting, or you prefer to be motivated and accountable in private. In addition, the Weight Watchers app helps you keep track of your food and goals on the go. Fitocracy is another website that focuses on exercise. There, you can turn your fitness goals into game rewards, unlocking levels and earning points. On both these sites, the built-in communities also keep you on track and support you as you work toward your goals.

Technology is changing the way we exercise, turning it into a game and making it fun. For some people, exercise is fun in and of itself. But for the rest of us, we need something external to keep us going and committed to a routine for the long term. By turning exercise into a game, we keep at it, trying harder, working out longer, eating healthier. And sometimes, just watching their parents get in shape can encourage kids (and spouses)

to join in, or even exercise on their own.

Kids tend to love video games, and making games available that require physical activity will really get them moving in their free time. Ideally, they would be running around outside in the fresh air, but we all know that things don't always work out that way. Sometimes our kids have a lot of energy when it is raining, or too cold, or too dark outside.

Another advantage of exercising with a game system is convenience. The best exercise regimen is one that someone will stick with. If, like me, getting out to a gym is more inconvenience than your schedule or situation will allow, you now have no more excuses. No matter the time of day, weather, condition of your transportation, or age of your children, using a game system exercise program is convenient. It is what got me to be active on a regular basis, and, in the end, was much cheaper than a gym membership.

Introducing Kids to Classic Video Games

five tips to achieving console harmony

 One of the things that define geeks may be our enthusiasm for our pastimes and hobbies. And that is no more apparent than in our desire to share the games and experiences of our childhood with our own kids. For those of us who grew up in the '70s and '80s, during the height of Atari and Nintendo, that means rolling out the old consoles and trying to convince our kids that, yes, *Frogger* is cool.

But it isn't always easy. Times change, after all. However, these five tips might help make the transition from the joystick generation to the touchpad generation a little bit easier.

Start slow. You can't expect your kids to throw off the Kinect and go all old-school NES in a matter of minutes. Games these days are so drastically different from when we were children that your kids will likely be skeptical on a first glance. Don't despair if your first classic games night ends with rolled eyes and boredom; remember, you've got a huge library to choose from. Eventually something will stick.

Lead by example. This holds true for so many parenting schemes. The things you love that you approach with enthusiasm will, more often than not, attract your kids like butterflies. You don't even have to make a big deal out of it. Just haul out your old consoles, and fire them up for a few minutes. See what happens. Curiosity is a powerful tool.

Think games in a broad sense, not necessarily just video games. I remember being really hesitant to play backgammon when my dad dragged it out one family outing. It looked ancient and boring. But before I knew it, the whole family was having a blast. It's one of the best memories I have of us playing games together. In some ways, old-school games are like board games in comparison to the tech that kids have these days. Let them know that times have changed, but the joy that can be had from games hasn't. Good games are just good games.

Go historic on them. Have they been playing the latest *Zelda*? Rocking it with *Mario Kart*? They might get a kick out of following the trajectory of the game throughout its mythos. Tapping into your kids' geeky interests is always a good way to go.

Be patient. You know your games are cool. And chances are, they will, too. It just might not be overnight. Remember, all things come back in style eventually. Just when you least expect it, you may all be staying up playing *Space Invaders*! Keep in mind that early games aren't so forgiving on players. You really only have three lives in *Mario Bros.* Use

the challenges as a way to engender some good-natured competition! Your kids might end up beating that level in *Mega Man* you never could.

Five Robots
i'd like to have in my home

A while back, I got the chance to try out a robotic vacuum for a month. It's not like I normally spend a lot of time vacuuming, but I have a soft spot for gadgets, and the idea of a mechanical helper around the house was oddly appealing. By the end of the month, that little programmable servant had become a part of the family. I liked hearing it rev up at seven every morning like a jet about to take off. And I really liked coming downstairs for breakfast just in time to see it backing itself into its recharging station, my floors dust-free. In fact, the machine shamed me into pulling out the upright once a week to touch up all the nooks and crannies the little feller couldn't reach.

Best of all, I liked that the Neato XV-11 was reliable. Unlike human teenagers, I didn't have to remind it every morning, and I didn't have to ask twice. And it never complained. True, it looked like a hockey puck, but I sighed when it came time to return the thing after the test period was over.

That experience got me thinking: What else could robots do to make my life better? The ultimate mother's helper would probably be a Bill Gates–style Smart Home that could anticipate all our needs. But as a start, here

are five robots I'd be happy to welcome into our abode:

1 LAUNDRYBOT: At UC Berkeley, students taught the PR2, an off-the-shelf research robot from Willow Garage that looks a bit like the Jetsons' Rosie, to load and empty a washing machine and fold towels. While I'm not complaining, what I'd really like to see would be an entire robotic laundry system. Something that could suck up clothes left on the bedroom floor, shoot them over to the washer via pneumatic tubes, sort, press, and fold them and return them to their respective owners' rooms.

2 ROBOCAT: Probably my least favorite job around the house is getting rid of animal pests, especially the rodent infestation that hits the attic every year when the weather turns cold. My Robocat would live up in the rafters, ready to pounce whenever anything smaller than my kids started to move. It wouldn't set off my fur allergies, or need cat chow or a litter box.

3 ANIMATRONIC SALMAN KHAN: Unlike many moms, I enjoy helping my kids with math—up to a point. And that point is called "trigonometry." Robotic teachers are already being used in classrooms in Japan and South Korea, and they should have no problem handling advanced math. So robotic tutors in the home seem like the next logical step. And what better personality to model them after than Salman Khan? On his website, Khan Academy, he's created thousands of instructional videos on math, science, and other tough subjects. If any research labs are listening, we could really use an Animatronic Salman Khan fast—I've got a teen who needs to start prepping for the SATs.

4 AUTOCAFFEINATOR: Using a sophisticated breathalyzer-type sensor to determine your blood chemical levels and motion detectors to see whether you're peppy or dragging, the Autocaffeinator starts brewing the exact formula to meet your needs. It can be programmed to dispense your favorite coffee, tea, or carbonated energy

drink any time of the day or night. A biometric iris reader could make sure your six-year-old didn't end up with a glass of mulled wine instead of warm milk.

5 THE WHAT'S-FOR-DINNERMATRON: Having to cook a meal at the end of the day is hard enough without having to figure out what everyone feels like eating on top of it. Like the Autocaffeinator, the What's-for-Dinnermatron uses special sensing mechanisms to pick out just the right meal for the entire family. No home-baked cookies though—much as we appreciate the help of our cyberservants, we moms still need to make sure we don't make ourselves obsolete!

CHAPTER 4
INQUIRING MINDS
WANT TO KNOW!

Bringing Science Home for Our Kids and Ourselves

Marie Curie aside, it has never been easy to be a mom and a scientist. True, the attitude that women are just not as capable as men when it comes to studying science has largely disappeared. But many women who start on the path to teach at the college level or do research still drop out before they reach their goal. So many, in fact, that the problem has been given a name: the "leaky pipeline." And the main cause? Motherhood. According to researchers at Cornell University, long hours and the lack of child care and other support are still barriers for female scientists and engineers who want to have families as well as careers. Happily, places like MIT are continuing to look for ways to help these moms make full use of their training and talent.

At the same time, these professionally trained Geek Mom scientists are looking for ways to share their excitement and enthusiasm for their chosen field with their kids and with other children. Kate Miller, who holds a master's degree in public health and a doctorate in demography, founded the company Charlie's Playhouse when she noticed a dearth of science toys. Other scientist/mothers have looked for ways to bring hands-on experiments to kids at a time when schools are lessening their focus on scientific discovery. Some have started websites, like astrophysicist (and *GeekMom* blog writer) Helene McLaughlin's site Lady Astrid's Laboratory. Others have created enrichment programs, such as Siena College physics professor Michele McColgan's Saturday Scholars workshops.

But it's not just scientists who are interested in science. Even Geek Moms who are decidedly artsy love learning about how the world works. They're the kind of people who sit down and watch an episode of the PBS show *NOVA* with their kids, just for fun. After all, where would sci-fi and steampunk be without science? Some moms are even joining the upsurge in amateur science and maker culture by helping students compete in robotics contests and science fairs. They're involving their kids in "citizen science" projects like tagging monarch butterflies, taking river water samples, or helping turtles migrate safely. Here are some ways you can share the joy of science with your kids, whether you're a brain surgeon or an English major who couldn't titrate a solution if her life depended on it.

Girls and Science

Girls love science—even if they approach it differently than boys do. I know from teaching afterschool enrichment classes that when you give a group of kids a challenge to solve or a project to create using science and math, the girls will be just as quick and eager as the boys. And according to experts like astronaut Sally Ride, who holds a Ph.D. in physics, statistics show girls have the smarts to do well in careers in these fields. But because STEM (science, technology, engineering, and math) subjects are usually presented in ways that emphasize things that boys like, girls often don't even give them a try.

Luckily, there's never been a better time to be a girl interested in science: from the Girl Scouts, whose "Imagine: Your STEM Future" program with AT&T introduces girls to hands-on science projects, to the NASA G.I.R.L.S. mentoring program, which pairs middle school students with women scientists, organizations around the country are looking for ways to attract girls to areas that were once considered "boy territory."

Research backs up some of my own methods of engaging girls in STEM pursuits. Some studies suggest that teachers—and even moms—may subtly let boys take the lead when doing hands-on activities in mixed groups, leaving girls to stand on the sidelines and watch. But when I show a class how to build a water wheel or wire up an electrical circuit, I go in expecting the girls to do as much work as the boys. (In fact, in second, third, and fourth grades, girls are often better than boys at putting things together, because they develop manual dexterity earlier!) By making activities like working with chemicals seem matter-of-fact, and treating the girls in my workshops as

competent, they come out excited and proud of their new skills and knowledge.

Of course, just seeing a woman who is comfortable doing math and science is good for a girl's self-image. Unfortunately, surveys have found that many female elementary school teachers are not. Girls need role models to help them picture science as a career that's fun and rewarding (and scientists as more than grim figures in white lab coats with bad hair). Some of my own role models include women who are playful and creative with science, like Leah Buechley, whose sewable Lilypad Arduino microcontroller has created a whole movement of wearable electronics. Or biomedical engineer Michelle Khine, who couldn't afford the ultrasmall containers used in cell research and made her own out of Shrinky Dink plastic sheets. There's also Margaret and Christine Wertheim of the Institute for Figuring, whose natural-looking models of coral reefs—made out of crocheted yarn using hyperbolic geometry—have been displayed at the Smithsonian's National Museum of Natural History.

Another way to attract girls to STEM pursuits is to show them how scientists and engineers help people live better lives. In a recent experiment, researchers discovered that girls were more interested in technology when it was described in terms of real-life applications—for instance, how lasers are used in plastic surgery. And girls want to know about social uses for science, such as the robots designed to interact and communicate with people by the Personal Robotics Group at MIT's Media Lab, founded by Dr. Cynthia Breazeal.

Toys can be a great means of introducing girls to STEM activities as many mothers of Lego-loving boys who grew up to be engineers can tell you. There's no reason girls can't benefit from "the Lego effect" as well. It's still a novelty to find gender-neutral and girl-centric STEM building sets and science kits in most toy stores, but this is changing. In fact, GeekMom's Andrea Schwalm created the "STEMmy" award specifically to honor some of the best of these toys that promote STEM skills in girls, such as the littleBits electronic sets designed by Ayah Bdeir.

Families can feed their daughters' natural interest in science by taking them to zoos, aquariums, planetariums, science museums, and nature centers. To show them science and engineering concepts in action, visit a local Maker Faire or Chemistry Week celebration at a nearby university, and stop for factory tours and craftspeople's demonstrations when you're out of town. Or encourage girls to sign up for more intensive STEM experiences like Space Camp, robotics competitions, or girls-only summer science programs. Even just sitting down and watching a science documentary researching a news item on space or dinosaurs, or better, bringing kids to a public lecture by a famous researcher or TV personality like the Mythbusters lets girls know it's okay to take science seriously.

Why does it matter if girls are interested in STEM? Intel Foundation executive director Wendy Hawkins put it best when she told GeekMom writer (and software engineer) Ariane Coffin, "Engineers change the world. They solve real problems. They improve lives. And, they live good lives themselves. The best way to make sure that engineers pay attention to the problems that girls think are important, is for girls to get in there and become engineers themselves!"

SOUND WAVE EXPERIMENT

This quick and easy experiment makes sound waves visible! It's fun to watch patterns appear in a sprinkling of salt or puddle of water, seemingly out of nowhere. Scientists call them "Chladni patterns," after the eighteenth-century German physicist and musician Ernst Chladni, who is considered the father of acoustics (the science of sound). Chladni patterns are not only beautiful, they're also used in the making of violins and guitars as a way to check that they are producing the correct vibrating tone.

Free (you have everything at home)

30 minutes

Age 3 and up

Easy

materials

- A recycled cardboard carton or box about 6" (15cm) across, preferably with a metal bottom, or a large can
- Any kind of audio speaker that can go under or inside the box, attached to a player
- Salt and/or water
- Plastic plate (optional)

STEP 1: Set Up Your Kinetic Sound Wave Display

Turn the carton upside down. Place it over or on top of an audio speaker. The wider the range, the better you'll be able to see patterns—although I have gotten this to work with my smartphone! If you're worried about getting water or salt on your electronic device, pop it in a ziptop bag first or cover it with a plastic drop cloth. You can also set a thin disposable plate on top of the box. On top of the setup, sprinkle a thin layer of salt or pour a little water.

STEP 2: Turn It On and Watch the Patterns!

Start playing some music over the speaker. Finding the best tones for pattern watching depends on your setup. Sometimes a nice low thumping bass will set the salt jumping or waves flowing in the water, but it may also respond better to a higher tone. The best results we've gotten, surprisingly, weren't from hip-hop as we expected, but from opera! If you play an instrument, you might also try this with some live music. Have fun and experiment!

SELF-PROPELLED BOATS FOR THE WATER SLIDE

We had a water slide in our yard nearly every summer when the kids were little. They had a great time but, eventually, grew too large to use it safely. Kids, summer, and water are a natural combination so I tried to find another way for them to have fun with it. Using a college class on boats and water currents as inspiration, I decided to use the water slide as a very crude wave tank.

STEP 1: Choose the Materials

A flat toy boat works well for this experiment but basically the boat can be anything that will allow for a duct-taped balloon on top. Keep in mind that the heavier the object, the more effort it will take to move and, thus, the larger the balloon that will be needed. Our converted Pinewood Derby car made of wood was heavier than plastic. It also was bulkier and not immediately suited to moving fast in the water. A toy boat has the advantage of a bow, which will help it go as straight as possible.

The first time I did this experiment, I used a bag of party balloons that cost $2 at my local grocery store. They worked fine, with a little trial and error. However, round balloons were harder to center on the boat. That meant they were more likely to send the boat sideways. A long oblong balloon propels the boat in a more forward direction.

Note: Keep any balloons or broken balloons, which are a choking hazard, out of the reach of small children.

The duct tape is self-explanatory. The boats go faster and longer on the water slide but the bathtub can be fun as well.

STEP 2: Duct Tape the Balloons to the Boat

We found this was easier said than done. The logistics of holding a blown-up balloon steady while using duct tape to attach it to the boat can be tricky. I learned to tear off the strip

$$$

$10-$20, depending on
materials at hand

Varies

Age 5 and up

Intermediate

materials I hesitate to recommend anything specifically save the duct tape, which is a must. We used several types of improvised boats, including an old Pinewood Derby car without wheels, a kid's toy boat, and a toy car. The balloons can be cheap, common everyday balloons that are blown up at home. However, trial and error proved that long, thin balloons give the straightest trajectory.

- Plastic water slide or a bathtub
- Duct tape
- Balloons
- Some type of boat

---

of tape before I blew up the balloon. Also be careful that the balloon is fully inflated before applying the tape. Applying the duct tape before blowing it up will prevent the balloon from expanding. That seems obvious but perhaps not to younger or overeager kids. Applying the tape with a rough touch could also result in the balloon popping. We learned to tape it firmly but carefully.

In our house, taping required two people, one to hold the boat and the inflated balloon and another to apply the tape.

STEP 3: Release the Boat

Set the boat in a part of the slide where the water is flowing steadily and let go of the balloon. Between water flow and the push from the escaping air, it should zip along nicely. Use several different types of balloons and several types of boats and that will teach kids a lot about friction and force in water.

A boat with a deeper draft (amount below water) takes more propulsion and will go slower. A larger balloon supplies more force and makes the boat go faster. And there's a big difference between how fast the boats go on the water slide, which has a current, and in a bathtub, where the water is static.

In the bathtub, just set the boat in the

tub and let go of the end of the inflated balloon. The boat won't go nearly as far but it's fun to watch and, if the balloon is even slightly off center, that immediately becomes apparent as the boat crashes right into the side of the tub.

The object isn't to find a boat that works perfectly, though that's always nice. The object is to let the kids have fun while teaching them something about water, friction, and propulsion.

And the many uses of duct tape.

GROOVY LAVA LAMP CHEMISTRY

I truly earned my Geek Mom cred the year my kids convinced me to tackle chemistry for our homeschool science topic. As an English major with more experience watching sci-fi movies than doing science labs, I found the thought of even boring old high-school-type experiments daunting. Luckily, I discovered that doing "real" chemistry at home isn't as hard as it looks. Using *The Joy of Chemistry: The Amazing Science of Familiar Things* by husband-and-wife science professors Monty L. Fetterolf and Cathy Cobb as a guide, I put together a "lab" using only disposable plastic dishware and household chemicals like aspirin and rubbing alcohol. Fetterolf—who told me he tested the book's demonstrations with his own kids in the family garage—designed the book to cover all the major concepts of a basic chemistry course, minus the math.

That was a good start, but I quickly discovered my kids preferred to see things moving, popping, bubbling over, and changing color. So I sought out chemistry experiments with pizzazz—and found quite a few that are safe enough to do at home. (A word of caution: Beware of any experiment you see on YouTube unless you can find a version on a reputable site, such as chemistry.about.com, Jefferson Lab (education.jlab.org), or Robert Krampf (of thehappyscientist.com), or from a school or museum!

This Groovy Lava Lamp project is a great place to start your explorations with home chemistry. It's simple to set up and carry out, the materials are cheap, easy to find, and safe for most ages, and it gives you lots of opportunities to talk about some common principles of chemistry, such as density and molecular polarity. Of course, how much jargon you decide to throw at your kids is up to you. But any way you do it, this activity is so much fun your kids might forget they're actually starting to think and act like scientists!

$$$
$10 or less

Under 1 hour

Age 6 and up

Easy

materials

- Tall, thin recycled soda or water bottle (label removed), 16 oz (half-liter) size or larger
- Water
- Food coloring
- Baby oil, at least one 12 oz bottle
- Effervescent antacid tablets (such as Alka-Seltzer)
- LED stick-on push light
- Plastic plate to catch spills

risk factor

Oil may stain clothing, so wear a lab coat, apron, or old T-shirt.

STEP 1: Prepare the Bottom Layer of Colored Water

The chemical formula used to make real lava lamps is a trade secret, but the gooey "lava" is a type of wax. And the way it slowly floats up and drifts down has to do with the balance between the density of the wax and the density of the liquid it floats in. At room temperature, the wax is denser than the liquid, so it sits at the bottom of the lamp. When the light is turned on and the wax warms up, it begins to melt and thin out, its density decreases, and it starts to float to the top of the lamp. Eventually the wax at the top, away from the hot light, starts to cool, becomes denser, and sinks down, creating a colorful display. Our homemade version uses water and oil, but the principle is the same.

Fill the bottle about one-quarter of the way with water. Add five or six drops of liquid food coloring. (Take a few moments to watch as the dye begins to spread in vibrant tendrils of color—the result of Brownian motion, discovered by botanist Robert Brown in 1827. Einstein suggested in 1905 that it was H_2O causing the movement of pollen Brown observed under the microscope, leading to one of the first proofs of the existence of atoms and molecules.) The final color should be fairly dark.

STEP 2: Add the Top Layer of Oil

Now it's time to add the clear liquid. Baby oil is mostly mineral oil—a nontoxic by-product of the manufacture of gasoline—with a little fragrance added. You can also use any kind of cooking or skin care oil you have on hand, as long as it's not too dark to see through. Pour the oil into the lava lamp bottle slowly, stopping when you reach the bottle's shoulder. Leave a little head room so the lamp solution doesn't bubble over. Let the bottle sit until the contents settle into two layers: colored water on the bottom, oil on top, with a nice sharp line in between.

The specific gravity of mineral oil (its density compared to the density of water) is about 0.8 to 1, so oil is lighter than water. But the reason "oil and water don't mix" has to do with the molecular bonds. Water molecules look like Mickey Mouse, with two little hydrogen atom "ears" sitting atop a larger oxygen atom "head." Those "ears" carry negatively charged electrons that give that end of the molecule a slightly negative charge. Oil molecules are nonpolar. They're made up of long chains of carbon and hydrogen atoms, which don't have a charged end. In chemistry, "like dissolves like," so the nonpolar molecules won't form bonds with polar molecules like water.

STEP 3: Turn on the Lights and Start the Action!

So far you've built what science teachers call a density column: one type of substance floating on another. To turn it into a lamp, just set the LED push light—a disk with three or four small bulbs embedded in it—on your plate and carefully place your lava lamp bottle on top so the liquid inside lights up. This homebrew lava lamp runs on chemical power instead of electric heat. To get it started, drop pieces of an effervescent (fizzing) antacid tablet like Alka-Seltzer into the bottle. Use as large a piece as possible—the bigger the piece, the more dramatic the effect!

As the tablet reaches the layer of water, it begins to release bubbles of carbon dioxide gas. (Fizzing tablets contain powdered citric acid and sodium bicarbonate, also known as baking soda; it's actually the same chemical reaction as the classic baking soda-and-vinegar volcano.) Because gas is less dense than liquid, the bubbles float upward, carrying drops and blobs of water along with them. When the bubbles reach the surface, the gas keeps rising, but the water drops back down to the bottom of the lamp, creating the lava lamp effect. The lamp will keep running as long as the tablets are fizzing. If your oil hasn't gotten too cloudy, close up the bottle and save it for another day. But don't put the cap on until all fizzing is over, or the pressure of the gas inside can create that explosion your kids are waiting for!

THE ORIGINAL "LAVA LAMP" EGG TIMER

The original lava lamp was created in 1963 by Edward Craven Walker, who got the idea from an egg timer made from a glass cocktail shaker he spotted in a pub in Dorset, England.

IT'S THE BLOB!

Every science fiction fan knows that crystals can almost seem alive. Under the right conditions, they can grow and spread faster than the mold on that three-month-old bagel in your kid's backpack. This salt crystal garden looks like it could qualify as an alien life-form, but the most exotic element in its makeup is an old-fashioned household product called "laundry bluing." These types of salt crystal displays are sometimes grown on decorative cardboard shapes, but for maximum weirdness grow your blob in a bowl and watch it try to take over your house. Don't worry about its menacing appearance; it's actually rather delicate, so keep it in a place that's safe from bumps and breezes.

STEP 1: Prepare the Blob Habitat

Salt already comes in nice cubic crystals, of course. But when it's dissolved in water, the salt molecules get the chance to recombine in different configurations. This salt crystal blob will take on a puffy or spiky appearance, depending on how much water you add. The sponge gives it a base to grow on and helps wick the salt solution from the bowl to the air, where it quickly dries and forms new fluffy crystals. To start, take a sponge, dampen it with distilled water, and wring it out. Then cut it into roughly one-inch cubes. Arrange the sponge cubes in a disposable bowl.

STEP 2: Prepare the Special Formula

Bluing is a suspension of tiny particles of a chemical called "ferric hexacyanoferrate," which makes clothes look whiter by tinting them slightly blue. Mrs. Stewart's brand bluing has been around since the 1880s and can still be found in some supermarkets today. Opinions differ on the purpose of the bluing in this formula, but according to the Mrs. Stewart's website, the ferric hexacyanoferrate molecules provide nuclei for the salt crystals to form around.

To prepare the special formula, combine one or two spoonfuls each of the salt, ammonia, and bluing. (You can leave out the ammonia if the fumes bother you, but your crystals will take longer to form.) Stir until all the salt is dissolved. Pour the formula into the bowl over the pieces of sponge. Then sprinkle two more spoonfuls of salt evenly around the habitat. Finally, squirt some drops of food coloring around. Different colors sometimes grow at different rates, making for interesting formations (and a good science fair project!).

$$\$$

$10

1 hour to prepare,
days to grow

Age 7 and up

Easy

materials

- Kitchen sponge
- Water (distilled water works better than tap)
- Salt (plain, iodine-free pickling salt works better than table salt)
- Ammonia (plain ammonia, not ammonia cleaners)
- Laundry bluing (in the laundry aisle, or at mrsstewart.com)
- Plastic cup and plastic spoon
- Disposable plastic bowl
- Liquid food coloring

risk factor

Ammonia can be irritating to eyes, and it's toxic. Be sure to use in a well-ventilated area. Use disposable cups and spoons for mixing chemicals, and throw away when you're done!

STEP 3: Sit Back and Watch It Grow

Salt crystal entities grow fastest when the air is dry. Under optimal conditions, and with the recommended materials, you should start to see buds forming in about an hour. And once it starts, you can almost see your alien blob growing minute by minute. Over the next few days your little blob should cover every exposed surface in the bowl and begin crawling out over the sides. (You might want to put that bowl on a plate to keep it contained.) As long as it's not jostled, it'll keep growing for weeks. It's up to you whether to keep it nice and moist or let it dry out a little between waterings. Don't let it get too dry, though, or it'll fall into a pile of dust. This is one alien creature that's really a softy at heart!

Home Chemistry Role Models

As the French Revolution raged, Antoine Lavoisier, the "father of modern chemistry," and his wife, Marie-Anne Pierrette Lavoisier, made discoveries about the nature of oxygen and hydrogen in a back room of their house on his days off from his job as a tax collector. (Madame Lavoisier carried on alone after revolutionaries marched all the

tax collectors off to the guillotine.) And in his memoir *Uncle Tungsten,* neurologist Oliver Sacks describes his childhood obsession with investigating different elements, with the help of his physician parents and metallurgist relatives. They helped him set up a lab in a shed off his family's kitchen, where flaming mixtures could be tossed outside into the garden, if need be.

MAKE SPARKS FLY IN YOUR MICROWAVE

Chances are you and your kids were taught that there are three states of matter: solid, liquid, and gas. But did you know there's a fourth state of matter—plasma—and it's the most abundant in the universe? Actually, with the Bose-Einstein condensate (a supercold state first created in 1995) there are now at least five agreed-upon states of matter, and scientists are debating whether there are even more. Some educators argue that such advanced topics should be saved until kids have reached the level where they can understand and analyze them (in other words, not until college-level physics). But as a Geek Mom, I say why save the good stuff for last? Introducing kids early to exciting concepts like hot, glowing plasma is the best way to show them science isn't just a bunch of boring facts to memorize.

That's why my kids and I made plasma in our microwave. Plasma is an incredibly hot, gaslike substance made up of charged atomic particles that generate electric and magnetic fields. On Earth, it only occurs naturally in the form of lightning, polar auroras, and extremely hot flames. But it's what stars, many other celestial bodies, and much of the space in between are made of. Amazingly, all it took to re-create this phenomenon in our kitchen was a grape and some oven-safe dishware!

Now, creating plasma in your kitchen can be dangerous, so I'll show you a way to see some of the effect with less risk. I'll also tell you how we created a ball of plasma in a glass that rose like the bolt of electricity on a Jacob's ladder (those buzzing rabbit-ear-antenna style devices in every mad scientist's lab). *Don't try this at home unless you're prepared to risk a broken glass or fried microwave.* And let your kids know that this can be done only under adult supervision. Make sure you and your kids are wearing long sleeves and safety goggles.

Under $5

30 minutes

Age 12 and up

Easy

materials

- Large juicy grape
- Knife
- Microwave-safe plate
- Oven-safe tall heavy glass, such as a Pyrex measuring cup (I used a thick-walled Pilsner beer glass)

risk factor

Letting sparks fly can leave marks or otherwise damage your microwave. Overheating the glass may cause it to break. Proceed at your own risk!

STEP 1: Prepare Your Laboratory

A microwave oven works by shooting electromagnetic waves through your food. You'll be making a path that encourages electricity—in other words, loose electrons that move around between atoms—to jump through the air from one piece of food (in this case, the grape) to another. This creates a tiny cloud of negatively charged particles, or plasma. It may take a few tries to get it to work, so keep extra grapes handy.

Start by taking a grape and cut it in half across its "waist," so you have two round dome-shaped pieces. Then take one of these halves, hold it cut-side up, and slice down into it, leaving a bit of skin at the bottom to hold the two sides together. Bend these two sides apart and place the piece of grape cut-side up on the microwave-safe plate.

STEP 2: Create the Sparks

To keep the plasma ball small, only run the microwave oven for a few seconds, otherwise the plasma may start to expand. If your microwave has a rotating turntable, remove it. Take the plate with the prepared grape and place it in the microwave. Darken the room if possible so you can see the effect better. Set the timer on the microwave for five seconds—but keep your finger on the "Stop" button. Turn the microwave on. You should see a couple sparks and a tiny fireball of plasma. Hit stop if it gets too big!

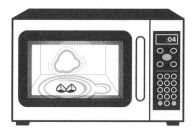

STEP 3: Throw the Switch!

If you're game to try the Jacob's ladder effect, prepare another grape on a plate. This time, place a tall, narrow, heat-proof glass over the grape. Again, set the microwave for five seconds, but stand by to hit "Stop." You should see blobs of plasma start to rise and hear a buzzing sound, just like in all those mad scientist movies!

BORAX CRYSTAL CREATIONS

I was looking for geeky decorations for my Halloween party one year, and I'd already bought a box of borax to make slime (for making ectoplasm, of course), so I did a quick internet search and discovered that, at least around Christmas, pipe cleaners and dissolved borax make for some intriguing crystal creations, usually snowflakes. As a kid, nothing amazed me so much as rocks and crystals, and it looked like a match made in heaven.

But what's a snowflake got to do with Halloween? Not much. So I did a little thinking and some tinkering with pipe cleaners, then went to work making my borax crystal Cthulhu. In my opinion, no good Halloween party is worth it without a little Cthulhu. As someone with a particular fondness for all things pseudopod, it just makes sense. There are lots of versions of this particular craft online, but here's what I did.

$$ \text{\$\$}

$5 or less, depending on amount of borax

30-60 minutes prep; 24 hours to grow

Age 3 and up, with adult supervision

Easy

materials
- Borax
- Large bowl
- Glass or plastic container (wide-mouthed is best)

- Pipe cleaners
- Pencil or chopstick
- Spoon

STEP 1: Prepare Your Frame

First, make your frame for the crystals to grow on. Remember that the crystals will swell the size, so don't make the circles/angles too tight, or they'll grow solid, especially if you soak them longer—unless that's what you're going for, which might be cool. Either attach a string to the finished frame or a spare pipe cleaner and then tie the end of that around a pencil or chopstick—you'll use this to suspend the structure in the borax solution. I kept it fairly obscure, arms and tentacles and a body.

STEP 2: Mix Up the Solution

Next, prepare the two containers: one for measuring out the quantity of water you'll use and another for the actual mixing. From what I read, this is to minimize crystals in the actual mixture.

Measure enough water to fill the container you'll be using for submersion, and boil it. I used my electric kettle and it worked pretty well.

Fill a large bowl (I used a mixing bowl) with the boiling water, and start adding borax. Mix as you do this, and continue to add borax until it's no longer dissolving (i.e., nicely saturated). A quart of water and about two cups of borax should do the trick.

Slowly pour the mixture into the plastic container and be sure not to pour in any extra crystals that didn't dissolve. Too many crystals will compete for growth later.

STEP 3: Let 'er Grow!

Submerge your frame, suspended by the thread tied to the pencil, into the borax mixture. Try to keep the tentacles/arms from touching the sides. (On my first attempt, both ended up touching and I had to pull them out, breaking the shape a little.)

Let the shape sit in the borax overnight, but feel free to check periodically. The crystals grow very fast, which is great for impatient geeklets.

And . . . voilà! The next morning, you'll see a sparkly, crystal-encrusted version of your design! A very satisfying, geeky, and rather unusual Halloween decoration for your party or your house.

You can also play with food coloring and different color pipe cleaners for a variety of effects, not to mention using glow-in-the-dark paint to finish off the creation if you want to up the spooky factor.

TRAVELING BACK IN TIME WITH A ROCK HUNT

We take for granted all that lies under our feet. But it doesn't have to be that way. With some science and imagination, a hike or a backyard excursion can turn into a time-traveling adventure.

Rocks hold the key to what once was. Sedimentary rocks tell the story of rivers and lakes, landslides and climatic change. Igneous rocks speak of volcanic eruptions. Conglomerate rocks are anybody's guess.

That's where the adventure comes in. While the details of geology can be a little overwhelming for the younger set, I don't think any time is too soon to introduce kids to the science and wonder of rock formation. Rocks really do speak volumes, even if they're silent. And seeing as they're everywhere, this is a project you can do on any weekend.

Depends on where the adventure takes you

Dependent on child's age

Ages 3–8

Easy

materials

- Lunch
- Ziptop bags
- Digital camera
- Imagination

STEP 1: Do a Little Research

Here in North Carolina, clay is king. In New England, where I grew up, it was all about the rivers—we even had fossilized footprints. Regardless, for your time-traveling adventure to really work, you've got to do a little planning ahead. Find out if there are any hiking trails with stratum or shale, and whether there's anything unusual about the way the land was formed.

STEP 2: Pick a Place

I could pick Hanging Rock, North Carolina, for example. And I'd find out as much as I could about it: how the land was formed with so many nobs due to erosion over time of a quartzite "blanket" that once covered the area; that the Sauratown Mountains, of which it's a part, are named after the Saura Native American; that there are many native plants and animals in the area. (Regardless of your choice, always keep your kids' ages and stamina in mind. You can still find amazing rocks without going far!)

STEP 3: Head On Out

Pack a lunch, or get something local. As you drive to your destination, have your kids narrate what they see in the landscape. Ask them what they think the mountains or rocks (or mesas, plateaus, what have you) look like to them. Work on getting them excited about the environment.

STEP 4: Hand Them the Reins

For the geekiest of moms, this might be the hard part. Ask your kids what they think—how do they think the land came to be this way? Prepare for: dinosaurs, bulldozers, dragons, and all sorts of imaginative answers.

STEP 5: Go Hands On

While they're telling their stories, or afterward, walk around the rock formations and slowly start to tell them the story as you know it. Keep it simple, and relate it to things they like ("This was before there were cars, Andrew"; "A rock bender would be at home here!"). Discuss what went into the kinds of rocks you see and what they're made of and how they give us clues to their age and history. Encourage your kids to speculate on what life would have been like throughout the ages, what sorts of animals might have lived, and what might still be around.

STEP 6: Keep a Record

Some parks don't mind if you take home samples of the rock—and if you can take home little tidbits of the different rocks, it's a great way to preserve the adventure well after your trip. If you can't take home any souvenirs, use your phone or digital camera to take a visual reminder. When you get home, make a physical/digital scrapbook and record both the stories you told and the stories they told. Each adventure results in a new "chapter." The more you travel, the more stories you'll have!

While this is a pretty simple introduction to geology, it sets the stage for future lessons. As kids collect rocks, they'll remember the stories from each of them; as they get older, they'll want to branch out from the names they called them, to their scientific names. Fueled by a child's imagination, it's a perfect gateway to science and apt to be a great learning experience.

Falling in Love with Rocks

a girl and her geodes

It was summer. And I wasn't interested in pet rocks. I was interested in smashing them. In turning sandy stones back into sand, in discovering geodes from the rubble in the street.

Of course, there was only colossal failure. Geodes don't typically show up in suburban neighborhoods in western Massachusetts, but I didn't know that. With each rock I smashed (with another, much larger rock my mom used to border her flower beds with), there was a possibility of magic lurking just under the exterior. Every time I got a rock to crack just right, I held my breath, looking for a glimmer of quartz amid the rubble. Did it matter that I nearly smashed my own thumb to bits, or that all I had to answer for my day's work were bruises and little piles of dust and sediment? Nope.

In spite of my failure to find a geode in my own backyard, my love of rocks did not diminish one bit. I started saving up and buying rocks, collecting them in little pouches, reading up about them voraciously, and pleading with my mother to buy me a rock tumbler (she never consented; years later, I learned how loud they were, and figure she was probably very wise in her decision to deny me). It seemed to me that rocks held the answers to

mysteries that, locked away under their hard exteriors, were things I could only imagine. Even simple, nonshiny rocks, which, at first glance, were hardly anything to get excited about, told stories of extinct rivers and years of erosion. Not to mention holding the key to possible fossils.

Around this time, my friend Emily gave me a fossilized fish (a *Diplomystus*) for my birthday. Oh, there were a lot of typical presents suitable for an eight-year-old that year: Barbies, craft kits, the like. But that fossil was something more. It was immediately cherished and sat on my desk until I graduated from high school, long after the glow of that summer wore off. It was a permanent reminder of what made rocks so special, a statement of the possibilities they held.

Because even if rocks don't speak, they have stories to tell. In an age of technology and virtual worlds, it's a constant reminder that truly amazing things lie just beneath our feet, if only we are brave enough to look.

The Gardening Geek

 I know where I got the geek gene, if there is one. There's no doubt looking at pictures of my dad in high school that he was one of us. He was reading science fiction, wearing horn-rims, obsessing about the Beatles, and nerding out over studio equipment before the word *geek* really became anything other than horribly derogatory. But my mom? The only geek genes she has are likely dormant; maybe she's a carrier. She's always been a social butterfly, a fashion trendsetter, and usually the most beautiful person in the room. Geek? No way.

But Mom did teach me something very important, and that's a love of gardening—whether it's for the joy of blossoms and fragrances (peonies being my favorite) or the promise of a harvest bounty. Sure, I don't garden the way she does. She's a freestyle gardener. Hard-pressed, she likely doesn't know the name of most of her flowers, and she rescues wildflowers from the woods and the side of the road. When it comes to her garden, no flower (or weed) will be turned away if deemed beautiful in her eyes. And all her flowers are girls, no matter how much science I try to throw at her.

My take on gardening is different. Though I wouldn't go so far as to say I'm an amateur botanist, I do enjoy learning the Latin names of flowers. Why say "columbine" when you can say *Aquilegia,* "hawthorne" when there is *Crataegus oxyacantha,* "lily of the valley" when the words *Convallaria majalis* are just so enticing to say? I could easily go down the rabbit hole, but then I'd spend too much time learning the nomenclature and forgetting to actually garden. I can imagine this is the fate of many geeks.

Thankfully, though, gardening is so much more than names. Flowers and plants are living lessons, their simple roots reaching centuries and traveling across the world. New world vegetables and fruits like sugar cane, cocoa, and corn all have astonishing histories connected to them, from feast to famine, from celebrations to sacrifice. Planting these crops ties us to the people who came before us, teaches us about the importance of preserving the environment, and promotes responsibility and stewardship.

These days it's easy to go high-tech with gardening, but I'll admit, aside from some gardening apps and weather widgets, I prefer the old-fashioned way. It's the simplest of sciences, really: sunshine, soil, seeds, and water. What makes it so geeky? My particular take on gardening means I seek out the strange and unusual. My mom doubted my Japanese eggplants and Swiss chard, but was delighted by their color and composition when they grew in. She didn't want to touch the okra I grew, but she called me to tell me how amazing the blossoms were when they came in. Maybe I bring out the geek in her, after all.

Growing Heirloom Fruits and Vegetables

 When gardening, my aim isn't necessarily to replicate what's in the grocery store. All those symmetrical fruits and vegetables have their purpose: they're easier for cutting and, at least among pickier eaters, they look nice. But all that homogeneity comes at a price. Narrowing down any gene pool to the point of so-called perfection just isn't a good idea in the long run.

The truth is that fruits and vegetables evolve on their own, and while we're accustomed to seeing green cucumbers and red tomatoes, it's really just a very small slice of what's out there. To put a definition on it: heirloom vegetables are allowed to propagate with open pollination. That means they're not grafted or grown from cuttings to keep certain traits (smooth skin, uniform color, etc.) intact. They still come in varieties, but they exhibit far more variety than the average, expected fruits and vegetables. And as far as taste goes, in my humble opinion, they far outperform their more predictable cousins.

My first foray into heirloom fruits and vegetables came in the form of tomatoes. I was at our local seed and feed store, perusing the seedlings, and noticed some tomato plants with vivid purple fruit, as promised by the label. Cherokee Purples, they were called. I took them home and quickly learned that, like many heirlooms (or cultivars), they came with their own history (apparently a gift by local Cherokees to farmers) and mythology. With names like Brandywine, Mr. Stripey,

and Fourth of July, just the nomenclature is enough to make you fall in love.

But tomatoes are just the beginning. Potatoes come in a rainbow of colors and shapes, as do melons, roses, and even corn. Even better? Because of their strong genetics, heirloom vegetables are often naturally resistant to pests and can survive some pretty nasty weather. Still, you've got to take some things into consideration with heirlooms.

Use your local seed store. You can find heirlooms at big-brand stores, but you're probably not as likely to find truly knowledgeable folks on the subject matter. You might want to grill your local gardening expert. They'll help you determine what best fits your gardening style and culinary curiosity. Not all tomatoes, for instance, are ideal for sauces or canning. If you're just starting out, you might want to try a mini variety, like Sweet 100s, which are plentiful and perfect for snacking, but require a little less in the way of care than their big, brawny relatives.

Use the internet. Yes, everything's gone digital these days. Heirloom vegetables have seen quite a renaissance of late with seed exchanges and special-order providers giving people access to difficult-to-find varieties of fruits and vegetables that they'd otherwise have to trek halfway across the country for. Try them if you're on the lookout for something truly unusual (purple broccoli, orange okra, green eggplants, or white carrots). You can also get large bundles of seeds and, since seeds last for a while in good, dry conditions, you can store them and use them again in following years.

Enlist everyone. Although many aspects of gardening are challenging for kids (the waiting!), make sure that they're with you every step of the way, and take their opinions into consideration. They'll feel a huge sense of ownership and pride when their seeds take root, and they'll be even more enthusiastic about eating the vegetables. My son can't get enough speckled beans and yellow tomatoes, and he's been helping us out since he was old enough to walk.

Scale appropriately. I know from personal experience that the lure of a veritable cornucopia of fruits and vegetables in a spectrum of colors is tempting, indeed. But raising a family and raising a garden can be quite the challenge. Make sure the plants you choose are appropriate for your particular climate, and be careful not to give yourself too much to do. There's no shame in starting small with a few seedlings and easy-care plants (like beans, squash, and root vegetables). If the gardening bug really takes off in your family, and you have the room to grow, you can consider grander plans in the future.

Take good notes. Not every heirloom or experiment is going to work. But many of them will. Your memory, however, isn't so reliable. Take notes each year on the harvest, planting, and process. They don't have to be detailed, but it'll come in handy the following year. You can also preserve the seeds of your favorite vegetables, for the most part, and use them again. If you start a journal, you can also get your kids to taste-test and record their reactions—if the tradition turns out to be a long-standing one, you can check how their tastes change (along with their perceptions).

Growing produce is one of the greatest lessons in life. Not only are heirloom fruits and vegetables perfect for teaching your kids about genetics, the environment, sustainability, and conservation, but they're also a perfect lesson about how deceiving appearances can be. We are so accustomed to thinking of edible plants as one thing (apples are red, broccoli is green) that kids, and many adults these days, have no idea just how varied they can be. It's part of appreciating the surprises that come in curious packages and getting closer to our own earth.

Seed Sources:

Baker Creek Heirloom Seeds: rareseeds.com
Seed Savers Exchange: seedsavers.org
Amishland Heirloom Seeds:
amishlandseeds.com

LOVELY LAVENDER, THREE WAYS

(just for mom)

Of all the herbs I've planted over the years, none are as lovely to me as lavender. A member of the mint family, *Lavandula* includes thirty-nine different species and has one of the most divine scents on this planet. In the United States, some of the most popular kinds you find in garden stores include French lavender and English lavender, and species range from deepest purple to icy white.

During my first pregnancy, nothing soothed me so much as the smell of lavender, and my enthusiasm has not wavered one bit since. While there's nothing that says lavender can't be enjoyed by kids, I think the relaxation benefits of lavender are particularly suited toward Geek Moms looking to put good use to their crops.

That's not to say you have to grow your own lavender and dry it; you can purchase enough for these three easy projects (one pound, which is a great deal, will cost you less than twenty bucks).

If you have a large crop of lavender, the plants need to be harvested, stripped of their leaves, and let to hang upside-down for at least two weeks before being used in these projects. Each variety is a little different, so check online for the proper harvesting and drying procedure before beginning.

I. LAVENDER OIL

I like this method because it requires no heat other than the sun, which is particularly good for the forgetful moms and busy moms among us. I've seen a dozen versions online that employ this method, which is a bit like brewing sun tea, but with oil.

STEP 1: Assemble the Jar

Slightly crush the lavender before pouring into the jar. This will help release some of the oils and components within the blossoms, as well as the color. Once the jar is filled, cover the blossoms with olive oil. Seal tightly.

$$$

$10-$20

1-3 months (mostly waiting time)

Adult

Easy

materials

- 1 large mason jar
- Enough lavender buds to fill said jar (about 2 cups)
- Olive oil (16 oz, doesn't need to be super high quality, but extra virgin will have less odor)
- Cheesecloth

STEP 2: Here Comes the Sun

Find a nice, sunny place to put your oil, like a kitchen window. Every few days, shake up the oil a little bit. You can wait anywhere between one and three months, depending on how intense you want the final outcome to be.

STEP 3: Strain

When you've got the fragrance you'd like fully achieved, strain the mixture with cheesecloth, squeezing to make sure you get all that goodness. You may need to strain it a few times to achieve maximum clarity.

STEP 4: Bottle

Store your finished lavender oil in a bottle of your choosing, or put it right back into the jar if you prefer. Lavender oil can be used as a personal fragrance, as a moisturizer, or as an infusion to potpourri, among many other uses (including shaving!).

II. EASY LAVENDER LEMON SOAP

$$$

$10-$30

1-2 hours

Adult

Easy

materials

- Melt-and-pour glycerin soap, 2 lbs
- Soap molds (total yield depends on mold shape/size)
- 4 oz lavender
- Lemon essential oil

STEP 1: Melt and Pour

Soap making can be a dangerous experience, what with the lye and all. But melt-and-pour glycerin soaps are a great alternative for those of us looking to save a few pennies by making delightful soaps we'd otherwise have to shell out five bucks a bar for.

Most melt-and-pour soap bases can be purchased for around five dollars a pound, which is ideal for smaller batches like this.

Following the directions, melt your base completely–typically in a microwave or a double boiler–and then add a few drops of the lemon essential oil. Some essential oils pack more of a punch, so check with the maker for potency. Mix well.

Pour into molds of your choosing.

STEP 2: Add the Lavender

Once the soap has cooled for about an hour, sprinkle lavender on the top. If you opt not to wait, the lavender will be more evenly distributed throughout. I like the layer of lavender because it works both as an exfoliant and delivers some maximum fragrance. Lather up!

III. SPOONFLOWER SWATCH SACHETS

$$\$\$$$

$10-$15

1-2 hours

Adult

Easy

materials
- Fabric scraps (two 8 x 8 remnants will yield 8 sachets)
- Lavender blossoms (¾ cup or so)
- Ribbon or yarn

I absolutely love Spoonflower.com, where you can design your own fabric and peruse thousands of designs from all over the web. But what to do with all those $5 swatches? Make sachets, of course! You can use quilting remnants, old T-shirts, sewing scraps, or any other suitable fabric. But I like the idea of putting a geeky spin on these with the Spoonflower patterns, which often turn up some delightfully mathematical and pop-culture designs. These also make great gifts, wedding favors, and stocking stuffers.

STEP 1: Cut the Swatch

The $5 swatches at Spoonflower are 8 x 8. So fold them twice and cut into four equal squares.

STEP 2: Scoop the Lavender

Put a hefty tablespoon of lavender blossoms into the middle of the square (dependent on your variety; if you can't tie the top, chances are there's too much).

STEP 3: Tie and Stash

Pull up the four corners of the fabric square and tie tightly with ribbon or leftover yarn. To prevent spillage, you can first tie with small rubber bands and then cover with the ribbon.

Stick in your clothes drawers for fresh-smelling fabrics for months!

SPACE, THE FINAL FRONTIER

host your own star party

Pull out your telescope and have some families over. Learn about the moon's surface, the planets in our solar system, galaxies, star clusters, and other objects in the night sky.

STEP 1: Choose the Date of the Party

For a star party, choosing the date is very important. The sky needs to be as clear as possible, and what you want to view needs to be visible that night. For example, if there is a full moon, other celestial objects will be harder to see. If it's summer in the Northern Hemisphere, you'll have a difficult time seeing the Orion Nebula. So choose what to view, learn when those objects will be visible, and pick a night with good weather. Planning the party for during a meteor shower will give those waiting to use the telescope something else to do as well.

STEP 2: Invite Your Guests

Who wouldn't enjoy a star party? The awe and wonder of the night sky, along with the science involved, will offer something for every guest. Invite a mix of children and adults, making sure small children will be well supervised, and remind everyone to bring weather-appropriate outdoor clothing.

Inviting your friendly neighborhood astronomer or astrophysicist is always a good idea, especially if the person has a passion for sharing his or her knowledge of the night sky with others.

STEP 3: Get Your Gear

Although binoculars are all that is required to see the moon, some of the planets, and a few other night sky objects, a telescope will allow everyone to see more things, and in more detail. A four-inch or six-inch reflector is a good starter telescope for those new to astronomy. If you don't want to spend any money, see if a friend or family member can loan you a telescope.

STEP 4: Set Up for the Party

Print out enough star charts for every person or family at the party to have one, making sure that nothing prints in red or yellow, which won't appear when studied under a red flashlight. Current charts can be found online on sites such as Skymaps.com. A good site for kids is spaceplace.nasa.gov/starfinder.

Free to as much as you
want to spend

30 minutes to
several hours

Age 5 and up, with adult
supervision

Intermediate

materials
- Star charts or a planisphere
- Telescope and/or binoculars with a monopod or tripod
- Red LED flashlights, or regular flashlights with red cellophane wrapped around them
- Green laser pointer (optional)
- Warm clothing (coats, hats, scarves, mittens, gloves)
- Hot drinks (tea, coffee, hot chocolate, hot cider)

special skills needed
Some astronomy experience for the host is helpful.

risk factor
Nights are cold. Dress warmly!

Align the finder on your telescope, making sure that it and the main lens are lined up. This can sometimes be easier to do during daylight hours. Consider putting glow-in-the-dark stickers on the legs of the telescope, so no one will trip over them in the dark.

Set your telescope outside at least thirty minutes before the party so that it can adapt to the temperature and prevent image distortion. Consider fitting it with a lower-magnification eyepiece, which makes it easier to spot objects and to keep them in the viewfinder. However, if you plan to spot double stars or study significant planet detail, a higher-magnification eyepiece would work better.

STEP 5: When People Arrive
As people arrive, have them grab a hot drink and head outside to the viewing

area. It will take a little while for their eyes to adjust to the dark. As they wait, they can study the star charts with red flashlights, since red light doesn't affect night vision. If you have an iPhone or iPad with an app such as Star Walk or Google Sky Map for Android, your guests can also use that to learn about what they are seeing.

STEP 6: Start the Party!

Once everyone has assembled and their eyes have adjusted to the dark, start by viewing some constellations. Identify common ones, such as Orion, the Big Dipper and Little Dipper, and Cassiopeia. Then locate a few more obscure constellations. Green laser pointers can be used to point to the stars, and everyone can follow the laser beam to the constellation.

Next, view something easy to find in the telescope. If there is a crescent moon, you will be able to see lunar topography at the intersection of the darkened and lit portions. Another good option is Jupiter. The cloud bands will be visible and, unless they are in front of or behind the planet, you can see the four largest moons of Jupiter (Io, Ganymede, Europa, and Callisto) that Galileo discovered in 1610. The moons are also visible through steady binoculars. Saturn is a very satisfying sight as well, and its moon Titan can also be seen.

Once everyone has gotten practice looking through the telescope's eyepiece, aim it at a more challenging target, such as the Orion Nebula, the Andromeda Galaxy, or a star cluster such as the Pleiades. (For more target suggestions, see the Messier Objects sidebar.)

TIPS:

- Practice finding the night sky objects the day before the party, so when the guests arrive, you look like you know what you're doing.

- If your guests are new to astronomy, make sure that everyone will have some understanding of what they are seeing. Supply context for your chosen targets, explaining such things as the discovery of the Galilean moons of Jupiter or the Cassini Spacecraft mission to Saturn.

- Work to keep the object in the telescope's field of view, which is easier at lower magnification. Since the earth rotates, you will need to adjust the telescope regularly.

- To maximize the possibility of a successful party, schedule it when major planets are visible. Jupiter and Saturn are especially satisfying to view through a telescope, so even if your guests have trouble seeing deep sky objects, these planets may suffice.

- Good star party etiquette includes not shining lights (or lasers!) in people's faces, and warning others if you turn on any regular lights. Also, make sure a stepstool is handy so shorter members of your party can reach the telescope eyepiece.

messier objects

Messier objects are named after the French astronomer Charles Messier (pronounced mess-ee-ay). He assembled a list of 103 deep sky objects in 1781. All of them are visible through good binoculars or a small telescope, if sky conditions are favorable. Each object is known by its number on the list, such as M1, M35, and so on. If you are getting serious about amateur astronomy, finding the Messier objects is a great way to learn your way around the sky. Some examples of Messier objects include:

M1 Crab Nebula
M31 Andromeda Galaxy
M42 Orion Nebula
M45 Pleiades
M57 Ring Nebula

Many Messier objects are identified on star charts by their Messier number. See how many you can find in your telescope! Or join a Messier marathon where amateur astronomers try to find all the objects in one night, usually in early spring.

M45 • PLEIADES

CHAPTER 5
FOOD
WIZARDRY

The Geeky Family About the Kitchen

Cooking may well be the first geek hobby. Think about it: the balance of heat and time, the delicate alchemy of bases and acids, the tender play of tastes on the tongue, not to mention the history written between the crumbs. It's pleasure and pain, a necessity made tolerable by Homo sapiens' advanced senses and marvelously varied diet. No two cultures are alike, no golden standard of "delicious" exists—and yet, almost universally, families all around the world work together to create food and gather around the table to eat it.

And while many of our mothers and grandmothers sought escape from the kitchen, recently Geek Moms (and dads, too) have rediscovered the magic of cooking. Recipes are no longer relegated to church swaps and bridge clubs; they've found their way to the internet—bolstered by amazing cooks and culinary personalities on television, like Alton Brown, Anthony Bourdain, Nigella Lawson, and Andrew Zimmern. Perhaps no one does the science angle better than Brown, whose show *Good Eats* sometimes views like a food-based *MythBusters*. Lawson celebrates the decadence and experience of eating food, reveling in the sensual journey from plate to mouth. And Bourdain and Zimmern expose us to food from all around the world, introducing us to the customs and cultures, no matter how truly curious. They all show us that food is at a crossroads. It's no longer about East meets West. It's true fusion. And our lucky families get to experience it together.

It's not uncommon to read about geeky families making sushi together on Twitter, or baking bread with wild-caught yeast (not to mention cooking wild-caught game), or testing out unusual recipes unearthed in attics and cellars. There's even a movement to embrace offal! It seems everyone's getting in the act of cooking.

But recipes aside, cooking for the geeky family is about collaboration, sometimes as far as from farm to table. Involving kids in cooking is a perfect opportunity for teaching. A little cornstarch and water? Magic goop! Experiment with them and demonstrate the differences between leavening: How do yeast breads compare to quick breads? How do their structures differ? Baking and cooking are worlds of opportunity that lead to questions and explorations of science, history, and culture. Not to mention it'll prepare them for life outside of the nest (I've heard many stories about boys gaining popularity in college due in no small part to their ability to cook an actual meal). Passing down cooking knowledge and imbuing the next generation with passion for great food doesn't just educate them, it creates tastes and memories that will last a lifetime.

How to Get Your Kids to Make Supper

 To me, teaching your kids to cook (and clean, do laundry, attend to personal hygiene, and all the other little tasks of civilized life) is one of the major responsibilities of parenthood. And not just for their own benefit. As the mother of boys, I feel a particular obligation to future roommates and spouses to train my sons to fend for themselves in any domestic situation. Of course, I also don't mind the fact that adding a "practical nutrition" unit to our homeschooling studies has meant fewer dinners for me to prepare! In fact, I'd call teaching the kids to make supper one of the more successful strategies of my parenting career. It's not as hard as it might seem, if you know a few tricks.

Teach them a few of their favorites. Why wait until they're older to pass down your family recipes? If your kids love your meat loaf or your father-in-law's spaghetti sauce, they'll be all the more willing to make it themselves when you're pressed for time. You can also appeal to their nerdy interest in how things work by reverse-engineering the box mac-and-cheese they're addicted to, this time with a "real" white sauce with cheese.

- *Entice them with gadgets.* You know your kids have been itching to get their hands on the microwave since they were tiny, so let them mix up some Cake in a Mug, an easy internet recipe that you'll both love. (There's a link to my own version on geekmom.com.) Or give them an assignment to adapt a "normal" recipe to the slow cooker, using a resource like Stephanie O'Dea's blog *A Year of Slow Cooking* (crockpot365.blogspot.com), which has everything from Rice Krispies Treats to Taco Soup. Still got that ice cream maker from your bridal shower? Put it to good use by letting the kids invent flavors no one has ever heard of. For even more gadgetry, check out Jeff Potter's book *Cooking for Geeks.*

- *Capture their attention with tie-ins.* Use your kids' obsessions as an entrée to the kitchen. When my sci-fi fans were little, they loved flipping through *The Star Wars Cookbook* to find recipes like Twin Moon Toast (a variation on "eggs in a nest") or TIE Fighter Ties (a faster-moving "pigs in a blanket"). I discovered one of my personal favorites—Fried Apples and Onions (with bacon)—in the *The Little House Cookbook,* based on the famous series by Laura Ingalls Wilder. And in his teens, my cineaste son surprised me by offering to make *puerco pibil,* a Mexican pork dish from the movie *Once Upon a Time in Mexico,* after he watched a demonstration by director Robert Rodriguez in the video's special features.

- **Make cooking a game.** Challenge your kids to design a menu using only what's in the fridge, on sale at the grocery store, or in season at the market. Or give them a set amount of money and see how much nutrition they can pack into a meal. While they're looking for recipes, you can help them practice their internet search skills by typing in the ingredients they want to use and sorting through what comes up. Or gather some cookbooks written for kids and show them how to use the index.

- **Set the stage for their takeover.** When your tweens or teens are comfortable cooking (and you're comfortable leaving them alone at the stove), make it easy

for them to step in and make supper when you need them to. Keep ingredients for their particular specialties on hand, pencil in "their night" on the calendar, or let them substitute cooking for their daily chore. Most of all, resist the urge to quibble when they don't do things "your way." If you want them to help out and learn to be self-sufficient—and you do, don't you?—then stand back and give them the opportunity to shine. Kids have a tendency to rise to the occasion, so put up your feet, relax, and let *them* call *you* for dinner for a change!

THROWING A HOBBIT FEAST

Hobbits, if nothing else, are creatures of comfort. There may be no better scene to illustrate this than in The Two Towers, *the second book in Tolkien's* The Lord of the Rings *trilogy, where Merry and Pippin, having just witnessed the destruction of Isengard, discover a trove of food and pipeweed, and happily tuck in without a care in the world. Hobbits remind us that even in the most bleak of times, a good meal can be magic.*

The origin of this meal comes from the early days of dating my now husband. We met on a MUSH (a multiuser shared hallucination, or text-based role-playing game) based on Tolkien's works—more accurately, we were both hobbits, and food figured in quite frequently to the scenes we did together. I wanted to create a bit of that IRL (in real life) and though we didn't have a lot of money, I put together a hobbit-inspired Ploughman's Platter, which we refer to as Hobbit Dinner (though it's really more of a hobbit snack, since it's pretty meager by Shire standards, I'd say). These days our son frequently asks for a "feast," and this is usually what I do to placate him. Better even, it can be scaled from simple to decadent and is a great use for odds and ends in the refrigerator.

$$$

$10–$100

30 minutes

Age 9 and up

Easy

materials

• **A good platter (a sturdy cutting board works well, too)**

• **Food as described**

STEP 1: Selecting the Menu

Some suggestions:

- Three to five good cheeses. Recommended: aged cheddar, Dubliner, Wensleydale, Stilton, smoked cheddar, Brie, Camembert, goat cheese (a good variety of tastes and textures is always nice).
- Enough boiled eggs for one per person at least.
- Pickled things: gherkins (sweet or sour) are always a good choice, as well as pickled onions. Here in the South I also like to add pickled okra. And I've been known to toss in some hearts of palm, though they're even more off canon than the okra.
- Meaty things: cured meats (salami, pepperoni, prosciutto, ham), patés (if you're lucky enough to live near Trader Joe's, you can find paté for under five bucks), leftover drumsticks work well, too. Sausages. Crispy bacon. You get the idea.
- Bread: one of the centerpieces of the meal. If you splurge on anything, have it be good bread. I prefer sourdough or a good rustic loaf. And don't forget condiments, either. In my book you can't go wrong with lemon curd, marmalade, or currant jam. Just don't forget the butter.

STEP 2: Laying the Spread

Since this recipe has very little in the way of cooking, all that's required is assembling the food on the platter (or platters if you've got a really big crowd). Even the littlest kids in the family can get involved. It's amazing how impressive all the ingredients look sitting next to one another, nestled beside jars and jams and butter. Make sure to have smaller plates for each of your dinner guests and the appropriate utensils and serving spoons.

STEP 3: Honoring the Author of the Feast

(Optional) Before eating, recite a few lines of Tolkien's poetry. I've always been a fan of Sam's troll poem (which talks about munching, of course). And there is, as always, "The Road Goes Ever On and On."

STEP 4: Tuck in!

Or is that Took in?

MA! THERE'S NOTHING GOOD TO EAT!

I will happily bake anything. But I hate cooking dinner. It's not that I can't cook. But preparing dinner comes at the worst time of day, amid taxiing to various after-school activities or homework or working late. Thus, it often feels like a chore.

I've learned to make do. I rely a great deal on the Crock-Pot and menu planning. But there are times when the day gets away from me, it's 5:00 p.m. and I'm confronted with the inevitable "Ma, I'm hungry! What's for dinner?"

Here are some food staples to keep in the pantry or refrigerator at all times. Gathering them should cost only $10 to $30:

- Flour
- Bisquick mix
- Eggs
- Milk
- Bread
- Oatmeal
- Pasta
- Jarred spaghetti sauce
- Processed cheese
- Various favorite spices

What these foods all have in common is that they'll keep for at least two weeks and some for far longer than that. (I'm not exactly sure how long that jar of store-bought spaghetti sauce will last unopened. I'm afraid to test that.)

The idea is to put food in a kid's stomach in a short amount of time. If this idea appalls you or if you're someone who absolutely needs a certain kind of dinner for your children, it's probably a good idea not to read the rest.

My first choice as a quick dinner is "breakfast for dinner." Eggs, flour, bread, and Bisquick mix are the makings of pancakes or French toast. If we're out of maple syrup, there's bound to be one of the following in the pantry: jelly, cinnamon sugar, peanut butter, or honey. On occasion, when desperate, I've been known to pour chocolate syrup over pancakes or French toast. Naturally, after the first time I did it, I received requests for it repeatedly.

Oatmeal works, even if there's no milk. Similar condiments/toppings to those recommended for pancakes will do in a pinch. And, of course, eggs can be poached, scrambled, and made over easy.

Quickie pizza is another kid favorite. Take a slice of bread, cover with spaghetti sauce, add a slice of processed cheese, and pop it in the toaster oven for a few minutes. It's not gourmet pizza but it's filling. English muffins and bagels and even the pancakes from "breakfast for dinner" can be used as a base. If there's fresh cheese on hand, all the better, but I'm including the processed cheese because it keeps forever and therefore is more likely to be in my fridge.

Pasta is another filler. I always purchase several extra boxes when it's on sale. Obviously, the spaghetti sauce can be used, but it can be topped with other things too. I've used olive oil and seasoned salt or other spices like powdered garlic, onion salt, and basil. Think out of the box. Even mixing Cheerios or other cereals with the pasta will do in a pinch, depending on the age of the child.

My children are so familiar with improvising that now that they're old enough they can do it themselves. I'd never recommend this as a regular healthy meal plan but, occasionally, it's a great deal of fun and removes the predinner stress.

HACKING SNACK FOOD

apple pizza and s'more pie

I am not a cookbook person. Instead, I have a gigantic loose-leaf binder filled with recipes I have cobbled together myself. To me, coming up with a new dish is a game. I score points for using up the greatest number of rapidly aging ingredients in the refrigerator, fulfilling whatever craving I'm in the grips of, and at the same time keeping the dish appealing to two or more of the picky eaters in my family. This results in quite a few meals that would not pass muster at some other mothers' homes, but frankly I can't worry about that. At my house, a meal is considered a success if everybody tries a little of everything, and nobody gets up and makes themselves a sandwich instead.

A lot of my ideas are inspired by things I've eaten and enjoyed elsewhere. With two kids and a husband with food issues, I don't get to eat out at exotic or interesting restaurants very often anymore. So when I'm in the mood for something different, I think about dishes I've tried (or wanted to try) at other places and see if I can create my own version. That's how I came up with these two snack hacks. Both are a tribute to my sweet tooth, although one is at least nominally healthy. Apple Pizza was based on a favorite late-night treat I used to enjoy at a little café in Greenwich Village, which I remember as sort of an open-faced grilled cheese with fruit. I love that it's a mash-up of dinner and dessert flavors. S'More Pie resulted from an obsession I have with the traditional summertime goody. We never seem to have enough campfires, so I took a tip from a local eatery that serves a DIY S'More dessert (complete with a cute little tabletop firepot) and created my own all-weather variation. The secret ingredient (a trick I picked up from Potter's book *Cooking for Geeks*) is Liquid Smoke. I'm not sure how you can call woody flavoring that pours from a bottle "natural," but they do. In any case, it adds that outdoor aroma that truly makes the s'more. The graham cracker crust is my own clever touch. Try my homebrew delicacies and see if they win you over too!

I. APPLE PIZZA

 Roughly $10

 1 hour tops (not including making your own dough)

 Age 5 and up

Easy

materials

- Pizza dough (I use a half-whole-wheat dough I make in the bread machine)
- Olive oil
- Grated cheese (mozzarella, cheddar, or a combination works equally well)
- Apples, peeled and sliced thin
- Spices (I like to combine the apple pie standbys of cinnamon, nutmeg, and cloves with the more savory and exotic cumin and cardamom)

STEP 1: Assemble Your Ingredients

You can make one big snack pizza, or let your kids make individual-size pies. You can even make this into little hors d'oeuvre–sized morsels. Once your dough is rolled out in the pan, drizzle on a little olive oil. Sprinkle on the grated cheese. Now cover the cheese with a layer of apple slices. Add whatever spices you prefer, and top with more cheese.

STEP 2: Bake and Enjoy

Pop the pizza into a hot oven (450°F) until browned, about twelve minutes (less time for smaller pizzas). With its melding of dinner base and dessert upper layer, I admit I sometimes make apple pizza my main course. Regardless, it's tasty, quick, and lots of fun!

II. S'MORE PIE

$5-$10   1 hour   Age 5 and up   Easy

materials

- 1 packet graham crackers (9 crackers, or about 1¼ cups crumbs)
- 6 tablespoons butter
- Dark chocolate chips
- Instant chocolate pudding mix
- Marshmallows (mini or regular)
- Liquid Smoke (in the condiment section of your supermarket)

STEP 1: Prepare the Crust

Melt the butter in an oven-safe bowl in the microwave. Crush the graham crackers in a plastic bag. Add to the melted butter and spread in a pie pan. Then pour enough chocolate chips into the crust to cover about half the bottom. Distribute them evenly.

Bake the crust at 350°F for seven minutes or until the chocolate chips are softened. Spread them with a spatula into an even layer. Chill until the chocolate layer is hardened.

STEP 2: Prepare the Filling

When the crust is ready, make the pudding using the pie filling directions on box. (I used one small box and about half the milk called for in the pudding recipe, mixed by machine for one minute.) The result should be thick and creamy. Pour the filling into the crust and spread around. Chill the whole thing until the filling is set.

STEP 3: Roast the Topping

To make the roasted marshmallow topping, melt the minimarshmallows in the microwave for about thirty seconds. (Be careful, they expand when heated!) Stir in about ten drops of Liquid Smoke. Spread the topping over the pudding. Then decorate it with more minimarshmallows and/or chocolate chips if desired.

Set the oven to broil. Put the pie on the top oven rack under the flame for thirty seconds or just until the topping begins to smoke. Turn the pie to brown evenly. Serve warm or chilled.

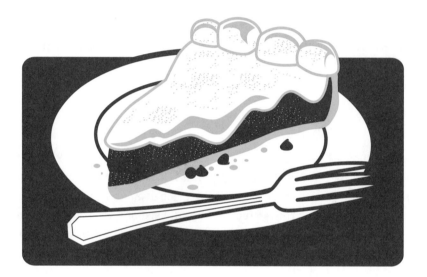

CAPTURE YOUR OWN WILD SOURDOUGH YEAST

One favorite family activity among Geek Moms is "kitchen chemistry." But did you know you can also try "kitchen biology"? This sourdough bread recipe began as an experiment in growing wild yeast as part of our homeschool studies on microorganisms. Although you can buy sourdough starter, in olden times housewives and bakers used to capture wild yeast from the environment. Aficionados will tell you that yeast captured in one area has a different taste than yeast found somewhere else—which accounts for the popularity of sourdough from San Francisco. We decided to see what kind of bread the wild yeast from our kitchen would produce.

We began with a method of capturing yeast devised by bread-baking fan (and microbiologist) Debra Wink. She did a study that determined that adding pineapple juice to the traditional flour and water keeps the starter's pH levels just right for suppressing bacteria and encouraging yeast growth. We created that first batch over three years ago now, and it's still chugging along.

Of course, keeping your starter alive takes a little bit of work. According to sourdough guru (and RPG writer) S. John Ross, raising a sourdough starter is like raising a pet. (Well, technically it's more fungus than animal, but the principle is the same.) To keep your sourdough starter fresh and lively, you've got to feed, water, and exercise it. That means pulling it out of the fridge once a week or so and giving it an outing (as explained below). We use ours about once a week for pizza or hot crusty loaves of bread. Of course, once you see how much easier it is to make home-baked bread with sourdough starter instead of store-bought yeast, you'll have all the motivation you need to take care of this pet!

To grow your own sourdough starter, follow the steps below. Within a few days you'll be ready to make the terrific half-whole-wheat sourdough bread recipe I adapted from S. John Ross's own classic original.

I. SOURDOUGH STARTER

$$$
$5 or less

4–6 days

Age 6 and up, with adult supervision

Easy

materials

- ½ cup unsweetened pineapple juice
- About 1½ cups whole wheat flour
- About 2 cups water
- Glass container with top

STEP 1: Start the Process

Creating life from thin air may make you feel a little like Dr. Frankenstein, but there's really nothing sinister, or hard, about it. You'll get the best results from whole wheat, which has its own yeast spores ready to grow. Once it's done, you'll be keeping your starter between uses in the fridge. A glass container is the least reactive and lets you see how your pet is doing. If the mouth of the container you're going to use is wide enough, you mix the starter up right in it. Otherwise, just use a medium glass mixing bowl.

Combine 2 tablespoons flour with 2 tablespoons pineapple juice. Stir the mixture well, then cover with a piece of plastic wrap. Let it sit for twenty-four hours at room temperature. Repeat these steps on each of Days Two and Three, adding another 2 tablespoons flour and 2 tablespoons pineapple juice to the bowl. By the second day, you should start to see bubbles. That's the live yeast, producing carbon dioxide. It's those bubbles that make the dough rise!

STEP 2: Nurture Your Growing Pet

On Day Four, stir the mixture in the bowl, which should be nice and frothy. Here's the part I like the least—having to throw some of the starter away. To keep the yeasties growing, you've got to give them some more food to eat, and get rid of some of the old stuff. But don't worry, once you've got your starter going strong, you'll be using every bit. For

now, measure out ¼ cup of the starter and discard the rest. Take the remaining ¼ cup and stir in ¼ cup flour and ¼ cup water. Let this new mixture sit for twenty-four hours at room temperature.

Repeat these steps for few days, until the mixture has doubled in size and smells like a brewery. Then put it in its glass storage bowl or jar and put the lid on loosely, to let any pressure from the carbon dioxide bubbles escape. Unless you're using it every day, store your starter in the refrigerator until you're ready to start baking.

STEP 3: Care, Feeding, and Use of Your Starter

Most sourdough recipes require you to reawaken your starter a few hours before you start to bake. The way to do that is to make a "sponge." I usually pull out my starter the night before and make a sponge overnight in a large glass bowl. That also gives me a chance to wash out the starter container. I loosely cover the bowl with a piece of plastic wrap.

To make the sponge, take the starter and mix in one cup of water and one cup of whole wheat flour. Let sit for a few hours or overnight. The sponge is ready when it's bubbly all the way through. The longer it sits, the more sour your dough will become. Measure out the amount you need, mix in another cup of water and cup of flour to what's left, then put it back in the storage container and pop it back in the fridge. If you don't use your starter for a couple weeks, throw some out and add more flour and water to help it stay fresh.

A layer of dark liquid may start to form in your starter. That's called "hooch." It's a little alcohol produced by the yeast (just like in beer-making). You can pour it off and add an equal amount of water in its place, but most bakers just stir it back in. It depends on how tangy you like your sourdough to be.

yeast experiments

You can also use yeast to do lots of fun experiments. Take a look at it under a microscope—the cells are nice and big, and if you're patient, you can watch them bud and multiply! Or take a little starter, feed it, and add enough water to make it very runny. Then pour it into a clean empty soda bottle. Stretch a rubber balloon over the top and wait. The carbon dioxide given off by the active yeast should inflate the balloon!

II. CRUSTY HALF-WHOLE-WHEAT SOURDOUGH BREAD

$5 or less

3-12 hours to activate starter, 6 hours to bake

Age 6 and up

Easy

materials

- 3 cups of sponge
- 4 teaspoons of sugar
- 2 teaspoons of salt
- 1 cup whole wheat flour
- 2 cups white flour (less or more as needed)
- 1 tablespoon of olive oil
- plastic wrap

STEP 1: Make the Dough

A big wooden spoon is a real asset when making bread. The more you can stir the dough, the less you have to knead. Although I personally find kneading relaxing, I try to keep it from becoming too much of a good thing! Measure out the sponge into a large mixing bowl. Feed the remaining sponge as described above and return it to the refrigerator. Stir in the sugar and salt. Mix well, then stir in the flour a half cup at a time. When it gets too hard to stir, form the dough into a lump and put it on a floured surface. Knead it by folding it and pressing it, giving it a half turn, and then repeating. Keep adding flour and kneading until the dough is no longer sticky but still flexible. You want the dough to stretch, not tear, when you fold it.

Then pour the oil into a clean bowl. Take the lump of dough, put it in the bowl, and turn it around until it is completely covered in oil. Then cover the bowl loosely with the plastic wrap and let it sit in a warm place for about three hours, or until it has doubled in size.

You can let the dough rise right in the oven, after letting it warm for a minute or two.

STEP 2: Shape the Loaf

To shape the loaf, take the dough out of the bowl. Knead the dough gently a few times, then form it into a ball. Place it on a baking tray. (I use a heavy baking stone.) Take a thin knife and make some gashes across the top of the loaf, so it doesn't tear as it rises. Cover it loosely with plastic wrap. Then let the dough rise again, loosely covered, for another two or three hours.

STEP 3: Bake and Enjoy!

Keep an eye on the loaf to make sure it doesn't rise too much. If it gets too flabby, you can repeat Step 2. When you're ready to bake, remove the covering and sprinkle the loaf with water. This makes the crust crispy. You don't need to preheat the oven, just turn it on to 425°F. Bake about 35 minutes, or until your bread is brown and fragrant. The loaf should sound "hollow" when you tap on it.

DUELING BREADSTICKS!

Kids take a special joy in destroying food. A breadstick fight not only satisfies this impulse but can also be a fun party game. Be a pirate! Fight with laser swords! Fight a mighty duel!

 $20

 1-2 hours

 Age 9 and up

Easy

materials

- Long, dry breadsticks, at least 4 per kid
- 2 bandannas or pieces of soft rope to tie one hand behind their backs
- A 4 by 4 beam or other narrow ledge on which to joust
- Pirate eye patches or Jedi robes (optional)

STEP 1: Choose Your Weapons, Set the Scene

The breadsticks can be found in grocery stores, usually in packs of twelve. The reason four each are needed is because the sticks break and crumble. With four, each child can have a full turn.

Tying the hands of participants behind their backs is necessary because, given how fragile the breadsticks are and how hard kids can hit, the fight would be over very, very quickly. Adding an eye patch will restrict their sight and make them look cool. (Well, it

should.) However, you could also cover their eyes entirely and make them duel with eyes closed, Jedi style.

If you don't have a beam or narrow ledge for the duel, instead draw an outline in chalk on a sidewalk or driveway. The important part is to have an element that limits motion and requires balance to win.

STEP 2: Begin the Joust!

Put two participants on the beam or on the chalk outline and let them go at it. The winner can be determined two ways. One, by who can stay on the beam or the chalk outline the longest. This will ensure that not only are the kids trying to hit each other with the swords but that they're trying not to fall at the same time, which should avoid the activity degenerating into simply kids whacking each other over the head with breadsticks. (They'll find this fun but it will, again, make the activity really short.) Or, two, determine the winner by whose breadstick lasts the longest. The first one whose breadstick crumbles down to two inches or less loses.

Then the winner moves on and the next challenger steps up. Rotate everyone back in until all the breadsticks are gone.

Other variations can be added, limited only by imagination. For example, if it's summer, dress everyone in swimsuits, provide the kids watching the duel with some squirt guns, and have them shoot at the duelists for extra difficulty.

Though this is a great birthday party activity, it's fun anytime because the setup is relatively simple, kids of all ages can play, and, most important to parents, it can get kids to use up their excess energy.

TETRIS CAKE

Think About . . . Cake Making as a Geeky Endeavor

Growing up in the '80s, video games were a huge part of my childhood. And, ultimately, a huge part of what made me a geek. Although many titles piqued my fancy and stoked the fires of my late-night obsession, perhaps no game is so iconic as *Tetris*. I was among the legion of shape-obsessed kids who were captivated by this curious Soviet import. This cake is an homage to hours spent humming along to the *Tetris* theme song and playing on my Nintendo late into the night.

Now, with the success of shows like *Ace of Cakes* and *Cake Boss,* Geek Moms today are attempting pastry versions of Death Stars, robots, aliens, or dragons left and right. However, as much as we might dream about making the perfect *Millennium Falcon* out of fondant, to the delight of our families, getting good results can be time-consuming and require a whole lot of skill and energy we just don't have.

So this recipe cuts some corners (pun intended!). It takes some standard recipes, like Rice Krispies Treats and sheet cake, and builds upon them. Rice Krispies Treats are particularly well suited to making Tetrominoes (the technical term for the blocks in *Tetris*) since you can get easy edges with a good, sharp knife.

STEP 1: Make the Console

Turn the thicker rice cereal treats from the 8" (20.5cm) square baking pan onto a cutting board and trim any edges to ensure a sharp edge all the way around. Since most pans are slightly curved, you want to accentuate the angles.

Trim about 2" (5cm) from the treat on one side, so you're left with a 6"-by-8" (15cm-by-20.5cm) rectangle.

Measure a smaller rectangle inside the rectangle, about ½" (13mm) from the edge. You can use edible ink markers for this, if you'd like, which can be found at your local craft store. Cut about ¾" (2cm) down all the way around the edge of the smaller rectangle. Remove all the treats inside the inner

$$$

scratch version,
$20-$30; store-bought,
$40-$60

2-3 hours, including
baking time

Age 5 and up, but
parents should supervise

Intermediate

materials

For the base:

- A one- or two-sheet 9"-by-13" (23cm-by-33cm) cake of your choosing (I used vanilla)
- 1 batch of Rice Krispies Treats made in a buttered 8" (20.5cm) square baking pan
- 1 batch of Rice Krispies Treats made in a cookie sheet about 1" (2.5cm) deep (this will give you a thin version and a thick version, with plenty left to share)

For the design:

- Enough black fondant to cover a 9"-by-13" cake (plus a little more if possible)

- Small amounts of red, green, orange, blue, and purple fondant
- Silver petal dust
- A pastry crimper (a little wheeled device that's great for scoring soft fondant)
- A clean, food-grade paintbrush (bigger is better)
- About two cups of buttercream frosting
- Parchment paper
- Good, sharp knife
- Cutting board
- Toothpicks
- Edible ink markers (optional)
- Small wooden dowels (optional)

---

rectangle, so that you're left with a lip all around the console piece.

Measure a rectangle 5¼" by 3¼" (13.5cm-by-8.5cm) from the cookie sheet (thinner) rice cereal treats, and make sure it fits into the main console rectangle. It's okay if it's a little snug, that'll actually help you later on.

Make your Tetrominoes. I cut the thin rectangle into quarters, and then used my eye to cut the shapes. (They're all made of four squares, hence the name; if you're feeling particularly geometric, you can measure everything out.) You'll need two each of the following:

- L-shape
- Square shape
- Line shape
- T-shape
- Zigzag (or lightning, as my son calls it)

Caveat: Don't use up all the treats, otherwise you'll end up with a failed Tetris (i.e., if you were playing the game, you'd lose because you filled up all the space)! Leave a little space for contrast.

STEP 2: Fondant

Everything now gets covered in fondant. For the Tetrominoes, color as follows

A note on Recipes

Scratch recipes are not hard to find online, and it's good to search for those that fit your kitchen capabilities as well as cooking skills. Believe it or not, the recipes on the side of most cake flours have always tested best in my book, as well as recipes from Ina Garten and Alton Brown. In my experience, fondant recipes that make use of gelatin tend to be more stable and smooth.

(Store-bought fondant is fine for the Tetrominoes, as long as you don't mind people making icky faces when they eat them.) Look for buttercream recipes that steer clear of Crisco. And, well, when it comes to making Rice Krispies Treats, you need look no further than the side of any box of rice cereal. Be sure to pat the treats down in the baking pan for a nice, uniform top.

(for authenticity): L-shape, red; square, blue; line, orange; T-shape, purple; zigzag, green. (*Note:* Parchment paper is your friend. It won't just save your countertops, it'll save your sanity. Put finished shapes on parchment, or even roll fondant between two pieces if need be.)

Feel free to make more Tetrominoes if you'd like. They're cute and people will enjoy munching on them.

You'll need to roll the fondant to about ⅛" (3mm) thick. Make sure the pieces are slathered in a thin layer of buttercream (dirty icing), and then cover. Don't worry about the backs of them as they'll be hidden in the console.

Roll out the black fondant and cover both the sheet cake and the console. The buttercream on the cake itself can be considerably thicker. Press down to make sure you get all the details of the lip you cut around the edge.

STEP 3: Detail and Assembly

Use the back of a knife to impress squares on top of the Tetrominoes. I also added a blocky look to the console and then used the pastry crimper on top of the cake to add texture.

Make your Tetris! Stack the pieces inside the console, anchoring them with toothpicks. Use extra Tetrominoes for decoration on top of the cake.

To anchor the console, I made a triangle out of two layers of the cereal treats and covered it with fondant, then leaned the console up against it, using additional toothpicks for support—it almost looked like a picture frame standing up. You could also place the console straight down on the cake, or use two wooden dowels (screwed into a platform underneath the cake) to slide the whole console down for a totally perpendicular presentation.

Dust everything with a layer of shimmer dust. It'll enhance the detailing and give it an almost plastic look. Oooh, shiny!

Sit back and admire. Then dig in.

STEP 4: Some Cool Twists on the Theme

- For the more advanced student, cast the Tetrominoes out of isomalt or sugar for a shiny, candy look.
- Stud the cake with metallic, edible beads.
- Write out the recipient's name in the Tetris font.

DIRTY ICING

You can't get fondant to adhere to cake without a layer of stickiness between. Dirty icing is a good way to do this. You just slather on the buttercream, usually in a relatively thin layer, and then drape on the fondant. This works on cereal treats as well as cakes. It's particularly helpful for getting younger kids involved, as they can get pretty messy with the frosting and it still does the trick.

CHESS CUPCAKES
& CEPHALOPOD CUPCAKES

Although big, fondant-laden cakes are still the rage, a stealthy and sweet second phenomenon is quickly taking over the cake industry: cupcakes. As a mother, I've come to adore cupcakes for their versatility and kid-friendliness. They're already portioned out, they're quicker to bake, and they're a snap to decorate. Not to mention, transport is far less frightening. It's also easier to do fun decoration without worrying about structure, so if you're a fan of box cake it shouldn't be a problem.

These two cupcake-decorating ideas spring from one simple base and make vastly different impressions.

I. CHESS CUPCAKES

$$$

$20–$30

2–3 hours, including baking time

Age 5 and up

Easy

materials

- 32 cupcakes, half vanilla and half chocolate
- Enough frosting for cakes, half vanilla and half chocolate
- Piping bags and large piping tips
- Cupcake baking cups (black/silver and white for chess)
- Stand mixer
- Good, sharp knife
- Scissors
- Cutting board
- Butter
- Edible ink markers
- 32 Popsicle sticks
- Sprinkles as desired
- Two sheets each of black and white sugar paper (check Wilton.com or your local crafts store)

STEP 1: Prepare the Cupcakes

If baking from scratch, I recommend setting your oven timer for twenty minutes, and checking at fifteen. The biggest mistake bakers make is in overcooking their cupcakes.

You'll need a total of thirty-two cupcakes. If you want to get fancy, half can be done in chocolate and half in vanilla, but it's not required.

Frost the chocolate cupcakes with vanilla frosting and the vanilla cupcakes with the chocolate frosting. Use a piping bag and a wide tip, like the Wilton M1. You don't need to pile on the buttercream; it's sweet, strong stuff. Start with the outermost edge and swirl your way toward the center.

STEP 2: Cut the Chess Templates

Using templates, transfer the designs to a sturdy piece of cardboard. Cut out with sharp scissors.

With a sharp knife or a razor blade—not for little kids!—trace two copies of each chess piece on the sugar paper; peel from plastic backing. Do this on both the black and the white so you have a total of sixty-four pieces.

Let dry for at least an hour. Otherwise the sugar paper will be too floppy.

STEP 3: Assemble the Chess Pieces

Lay out one cut chess piece and place a Popsicle stick on top of it, so it looks like a chess lollipop (making sure the stick doesn't go all the way to the top). Lightly brush the edges with water and lay the second, matching piece, on top of the first. Press around the edges to seal.

Allow each to rest at least a half hour.

STEP 4: Insert into Cupcakes

The black chess pieces go on the chocolate frosted cupcakes, and the white on the vanilla. Assemble on opposing sides!

STEP 5: Play with Your Food!

If you're feeling particularly adventurous, find a chessboard big enough for the cupcakes or make one of your own (you could use fondant or black and white tiles). I'd suggest actually playing a game with the cupcakes, but I know from experience they don't tend to last that long! Otherwise, just enjoy.

COPY AT 100%

II. CEPHALOPOD CUPCAKES

$$$

$30

2-3 hours,
including baking time

Age 5 and up

Easy

materials

- Two dozen cupcakes of your choice
- Enough frosting for cakes, in eldritch green
- Piping bags and large piping tips
- Silver cupcake baking cups
- Stand mixer
- Good, sharp knife
- Scissors
- Cutting board
- 24 Popsicle sticks
- Sprinkles as desired
- Edible ink markers
- Marzipan (two containers, store-bought)
- Petal dust in silver, spring green, and dark green
- Paintbrush

STEP 1: Prepare the Cupcakes

As with the chess cupcakes, if you're baking from scratch, bake them for twenty minutes, and check at fifteen, to avoid overcooking. This time, frost the cupcakes with green frosting. Use the same piping bag as before (a wide tip, like the Wilton M1), go lightly with the buttercream, and start at the edge and swirl your way toward the center.

Note: We are making cephalopod arms, not tentacles. It's a common misconception that the elongated paddlelike appendages of cephalopods that have suckers (like on an octopus) are called tentacles. But the cephalopod appendages are arms, not tentacles; the arms have suckers but tentacles typically have suckers only on the tips. It's possible to make tentacles, but they are very delicate and not really suited for this recipe.

STEP 2: Form the Arms

Marzipan is sugar and almond paste, commonly used in Europe to make intricate fruits and vegetable shapes for candies and decor. Although you can make it at home, this recipe requires so little of it, it's just as well to go store-bought. I'm fond of Odense, which has only three ingredients, all of which I can pronounce.

Start about halfway up the Popsicle stick (varying will give your arms different levels of "flop"). Work the marzipan for about thirty seconds until it's pliable, then roll it out until it's about 3" (7.5cm) long and about 3/4" (2cm) thick. Shape it around the Popsicle stick, tapering the end.

Again, this will look a bit like a lollipop. The top should flop toward you.

STEP 3: Dust the Arms

Using the petal dust, cover one side of the arms with dark green, and the inner light green. With the markers (in green or black), draw little circles to represent the suckers on the lighter green side. This is particularly good for younger kids since the petal dust doesn't quite require the same level of precision. Every squid's a little different, after all.

Set aside on parchment paper and let dry to retain the shape. Make enough for each cupcake.

STEP 4: Insert the Arms

Stick the arms down into the cupcake tops. You can make smaller versions with toothpicks and less marzipan if you want more arms sticking out of various cupcakes. If you don't have marzipan, you can use fondant.

STEP 5: Eat, If You Can!

In the past, I've added Elder Signs by applying stars in blue royal icing to chocolate pastilles, which gives the cupcakes a decidedly Lovecraftian air. If you're good with sugar, you can always add some spun sugar. I find sprinkles work fine to add an otherworldly tinge!

CREAMY FUDGE FROM ATOP MOUNT OLYMPUS

Mount Olympus was the home of the mythical Greek gods, with Zeus as the father. The gods would gather there to have meetings, and to consume nectar, ambrosia, and, in my imagination, fudge. Olympus was thought to be higher than any other peak; some say it was even located in the heavens. Regardless of its location, it was situated much higher than the land of the mortals. It is also likely that if they ever made fudge, the gods had to revise their recipe to allow for the difference in air pressure that accompanies elevation.

The first time I made fudge in our high-elevation town, I didn't think to make any modifications. I ended up with an incredibly firm, impossible-to-stir mess of dry but tasty chocolate gunk. The recipe didn't mention the need to modify cooking temperature due to altitude, and I didn't know enough to look into the concept. But, since water boils at a different temperature depending on air pressure, it makes sense that a recipe that depends so much on temperature would be similarly affected.

So, before the next time I attempted the fudge, I used science to turn a previously useless recipe into a useful one and ended up with a delicious confection with a perfect consistency. What follows are directions for how to determine your own formula for making fudge, whatever your altitude.

$$$

$5–$15

15 minutes for experiment, 30–45 minutes for fudge

Teens and up

Intermediate

materials
• Candy thermometer

• Saucepan, at least a two-quart size
• Water

STEP 1: Boil Water

Bring water to a full, rolling boil in the saucepan. Put your candy thermometer in the water, and read its final temperature. This is the temperature at which water boils in your location, for the given day's air pressure. Though many people believe that it is altitude itself that affects the boiling point of water, it is actually only affected by air pressure. But since air pressure generally goes down as altitude increases, the two are related. Since air pressure in any given location also varies with the weather, the boiling point there can also vary from day to day, though usually not enough to affect recipes. Figuring your location's boiling point of water on a day with typical weather will likely suffice for all future candy endeavors.

At 29.92 inches of mercury (1013 millibars), the standard pressure at sea level, water boils at 212°F (100°C). For my slightly-above-mile-high location, water boils at approximately 201°F (93.9°C).

STEP 2: Modify Fudge Recipe

Your chosen fudge recipe will state a temperature at which to stop cooking the sugar mixture. Subtract from that temperature the number of degrees below 212°F (100°C) that water boils at your location. The new temperature will be your desired final temperature for the recipe.

STEP 3: Make Fudge!

Using your favorite fudge recipe and your calculations, make your fudge. When others are amazed at how well it turned out at high altitude, be sure to share the science behind your results!

Why Julia Child Is a Hero to All of Us

 Julia Child was the first female geek to not only be famous but also loved.

She never set out to be a star. She certainly doesn't fit the image of a television host. But watch any of her old shows and she has presence. Child, a middle-aged woman with a unique voice, dominates the screen and seems excited to be talking to those who are watching. And we were excited to be watching.

Why do I classify her as a geek? Because she followed her passions and brought the rest of us with her.

It's clear from how Julia Child lived her life that she didn't want to fit into any particular mold. In an era when many women weren't educated, she went to college. In an era when many women never went outside the home for a job, she found a career in intelligence work. In an era when most women were happy to play hostess for their husbands, she wanted more.

What she found was cooking, in particular, French cooking. And she was so passionate and, yes, so incredibly geeky about it that she changed the American perception of food. It wasn't just the book *Mastering the Art of French Cooking*, which she spent years working on with her coauthors. It was her role on television as a teacher that won America over.

She loved what she was doing, and she loved sharing it with the world.

The French Chef, which began on PBS in 1963, won an Emmy Award, the first for an educational show, and Child continued to be on the air in one form or another for thirty years. She became so indelible that even a parody of her show in a *Saturday Night Live* skit by Dan Aykroyd became famous.

And all this fame came from following her passion, even when it seemed her book would never be published. She's an inspiration because she never let failure overtake her passion.

A Love Letter to Alton Brown

The first time I saw you, bespectacled and Hawaiian shirted, you were talking about mushrooms. Not just how good they taste, but how they ought to be treated in the kitchen. I watched, rapt, as you deftly discussed and dispelled the long-held belief that water and mushrooms just don't mix. With science.

Geek that I am, I'd long held that the key to good food is good science. After all, time, temperature, and chemistry are all part of the bedrock of great cuisine (dare I say, good eats). And you didn't just mention this in passing. No, you stuck to your guns through every episode, insisting on a scientific approach to cooking in general. Always use a thermometer. Just walk away. From sock puppet yeast to rubbery gluten models, you appealed to the kid in me by teaching through visual aids and (always) a wacky sense of humor.

Before you, there was the *Joy of Cooking*, my bible. It was the place I went whenever I needed inspiration. But you took those principles and illuminated them in a way for which I will forever be indebted. That roast chicken my sister makes whenever she gets a chance? She credits me, but it's your technique. Those Swedish meatballs that aren't my grandmother's recipe? Yup, yours, too. The scones my son can't stop eating? Ditto.

Now that my son is old enough to start his apprenticeship in the kitchen, he's caught the *Good Eats* bug, as well. At four years old,

he asked for bouillabaisse at a restaurant, and I can thank you for that. You've also helped me, a Yankee transplanted to the South, understand the history behind cuisine south of the Mason-Dixon Line, which has come in handy with the in-laws.

And all this is not even to mention the Chocolate Chip Cookie #10 recipe. I know it's not magic, but those cookies are as close to it as I might ever get on this earth. So thank you. Know that you have fans who are forever changed, and who can't wait to see what you do next.

With love and science,
Natania

Ten Essential Seasonings

staples for maximum flavor

 You can perfectly cook any roast or flawlessly execute a delicate flan, but if you've seasoned it wrong or inadequately, you'll end up with a flat and uninspiring dish. Food, both savory and sweet, absolutely comes alive with the proper application of seasoning and a handful of "backbone" ingredients. The following list, though not completely comprehensive, is a great start (for instance, I don't list Mexican seasonings, but you'll find cumin, turmeric, chili pepper, and oregano listed among the other "kits").

1 KOSHER SALT: Kosher salt is far less "salty" than iodized salt and enhances flavor rather than drowning it in a briny blanket. It's also ideal for baking, and it can even be used as a cooking vessel: you can cook roasts in a thick crust of kosher salt, seasoning it every step of the way. This is my all-purpose salt.

2 PEPPER: Throw away any pepper you have that's preground and in a tin. Real peppercorns have a thousand times more flavor, imparting sweetness, heat, and complexity to food that makes table pepper taste like ash in comparison. There are many varieties of peppercorns, from pink to white to black (depending on variety and processing). Pepper is an integral part of good dry rubs for meat and marinades, and it adds extra bite to vegetables and salads.

3 SPECIALTY SALTS: If you like to make dry rubs or want to really ramp up flavor, I recommend splurging on some specialty salts. Some of my favorites include the famed fleur de sel (sea salt harvested by hand in Brittany) as a finishing salt, salish (alderwood smoked salt from the Pacific Northwest) for rubs and marinades, and Himalayan salt (a beautiful pink, complex, mineral salt that is mined and can be made into bowls or lamps) for all-purpose cooking—it's particularly delicious on eggs. These can be found at specialty grocers or, of course, online.

4 ITALIAN HERB KIT (DRY): Don't go for the premixed varieties; otherwise you can't change the ratios and experiment. Basil and oregano are what most people consider the staples of Italian cooking, but I also include red pepper flakes, marjoram, and thyme. Where's the parsley? I'd not recommend anything but the fresh variety.

5 HERBES DE PROVENCE: There is no tried and true recipe for herbes de Provence, a classic pairing of French dried herbs. In this case, getting a premade mix is probably the way to go. Typically it consists of tarragon, thyme, rosemary, mint, chervil, oregano, and bay; sometimes you'll find it with added lavender. Particularly lovely on vegetables and lighter meats, fish, and poultry.

6 EASTERN FLAVOR KIT: In this house, we're big fans of the bold, clean flavors prominent in many Asian countries, particularly in Thai food and Indian food. Things I don't go without for Thai food: fish sauce, fresh basil and cilantro, ginger, soy sauce, and chili paste. For Indian food: cardamom, turmeric, cumin, cayenne, chili pepper, along with mixes like garam masala and other curries.

7 COMFORTING SPICE KIT: Comfort spices are among the most cherished, and I almost always exclusively go whole in this case. Many of these traditionally "holiday" spices are high in oils and don't keep for long periods if they're preground. The exception is cinnamon, which I usually go through fast enough. Whole comfort spices include nutmeg, allspice, clove, and ginger.

8 CITRUS KIT: Always fresh. Lemon and orange rind, unsung heros in flavor and freshness, bring new depth and dimension to food. The moment I started putting lemon rind into my cranberry muffins, a whole new world opened up. What one scant teaspoon of essential oil–laden rind can do for a dish is nothing short of miraculous. Just make sure you've got a good micrograter (also comes in handy with the nutmeg).

9 COCOA: I suggest both natural cocoa and Dutch process (which reduces the acidity) in your pantry, since you can use either depending on recipes. I typically go with natural cocoa, especially in hot chocolate, but when in doubt consult the recipe. I've found better results shying away from "big chocolate" brands (i.e., ones that make candy bars). Cocoa, due to its fat content, can go stale quickly, so avoid bulk purchases.

10 VANILLA: Another backbone ingredient. Good vanilla can make or break a dish. While it's not possible for everyone to afford top-of-the-line vanilla beans, I do recommend buying them if you're able, or at least using them in special dishes (like crème brûlée). Stay away from artificial flavorings, and if you're an avid baker like I am, stock up on real vanilla extract at your local warehouse store. Kept in a cool, dry place, closed tightly, it'll last a while.

SAVORING THE SMELL AND TASTE OF LOOSE TEA

I'm addicted to loose tea. And I've roped my son into it.

Shifting to loose tea from teabags was originally an attempt to gain more flavor after I cut out the two heaping teaspoonfuls of sugar in my morning mug. The reason loose tea has more flavor than tea in teabags is that the strainer allows the leaves to expand, thus providing more flavor to the water.

While I knew there was a wide variety of loose teas, I was astonished at exactly how many choices existed. I've tried flavors from key lime to maple syrup to chocolate chai to Irish breakfast with my son.

Loose tea looks complicated. It's not. All you need is a mug, a tea strainer, and at least an ounce of loose tea leaves. But, preferably, it's good to have various flavors of tea leaves available for contrast. Depending on price and amount purchased, that can be expensive. A normal month's supply for me is about $25. Pricier tea blends can be over $10 per ounce, however.

Education is so often visual or aural. Tea is all about smell and taste, and that makes it a unique activity for children.

There are three basic types of teas: black, green/herbal, and white. Black teas have the heartiest flavor and often the most caffeine. Green or herbal teas often have little caffeine and flavors often based on fruits or herbs and spices. White teas have the most delicate flavors and aromas. Chai is often said to be a type of tea. At heart, it's a black tea with spices. It's also a base name for tea in many parts of the world and can often refer to a spiced tea mixed with milk.

My son's first experience with loose tea was when we walked into a Teavana at the local mall. Teavana is a chain store and has many samples available for tasting but, unfortunately, they don't usually have samples of the tea to browse and smell. They're all behind the front desk and can seem a confusing array of green, black, white, and chai teas. Employees will pull down the tins to smell but that's not ideal for children.

My recommendation would be either to find a local tea shop—we're lucky enough to have one near us—or go to an internet tea store such as The Tea Table (theteatable .com). Our local store has all the tea canisters available for browsing, so every flavor can be smelled. My son loves going there because of that.

The Tea Table allows ordering of up to three small samples with each order, no matter what the cost of the order. For $10 plus shipping, you could receive up to four different flavors of tea, so it's an excellent deal. Teavana is more expensive and has no free loose tea samples as a general rule. Both companies will have strainers of various types available.

Once you have the tea, set all the flavors out on the table and start smelling. Decide what smells the best or most intriguing to you. Don't feel like you have to stick with the teas as is. They can be combined to form your own blend. Want a little blueberry kick with your English breakfast tea? Mix them. Want a little honey flavor with the spiced chai? Mix the types.

Try buying teas with out-of-the-box flavors. We found a popcorn tea at our local shop. That didn't turn out to be very tasty, but we love the key lime tea, which contains small pieces of fruit. The maple syrup tea has little maple syrup crystals that melt in the hot water of the tea.

Once a decision is made on the type of tea to try, boil up some water, put a teaspoon of tea into the strainer, and pour the boiled water over the tea. Let stand about three to five minutes but no longer than that. I like my tea strong and black. To get a less intense flavor, shorten the steeping time.

Then sip to taste. I add milk to most teas but herbal teas, especially those that are fruit based, often don't need an addition. Honey, cream, and sugar can also be added.

The great part about tea is that it has incredible flavor and few calories, making it a great beverage for children. The only catch is that tea can be a diuretic and cause trips to the bathroom. For children, start with small amounts to see how they react.

Often, there are medicinal claims made on behalf of some type of tea, usually an herbal blend. I take these with a grain of salt and instead follow my nose. If it smells and tastes good, then it's inherently stress relieving.

CHAPTER 6
MAKE IT SEW!
AND OTHER
GEEK CRAFTS

Taking Traditional Crafts
into New Galaxies

Women have always been at the epicenter of crafts, but in the last decade, perhaps more than any other, geeks around the globe have been doing more than traditional crafts like knitting, sewing, and jewelry making: they've been transforming the crafting movement, reclaiming it, and, quite frankly, going where no one has gone before. They're using crafts to express their interest in history, their connection to fandom, and as tools for educating their kids.

Take Ravelry.com, an enormous online community of fiber artists boasting two million users. From its launch in 2007 it's been a hub for unusual crafts. Sure, you can find plenty of garden-variety knitting and crochet projects there, and it's ideal for those looking to start a fiber arts adventure. But what sets *Ravelry* apart from more traditional communities is the unusual, and often geeky, projects shared by members. Here you'll find crafters dedicated to re-creating every single Dr. Who scarf by hand, immaculate reproductions of knitwear from the costumes of Peter Jackson's *The Lord of the Rings* series, Jayne hats, and Totoro toys for kids, predominantly designed and supported by women. These patterns make the rounds and are shared and commented upon; it's crafts gone massively social, taken out of the traditional fireside environment and into the World Wide Web.

But it's not just fan art that's risen to the forefront of the crafting movement. The handiwork is nothing short of astonishing, and often these talented artists seek old-school methods like tanning their own leather, working with plant-based dyes, and beading elaborate bodices by hand just to get the look right. There is a truly astonishing level of skill involved, with a great debt to and respect for our predecessors. At the same time, crafts are moving into the future, with conductive thread and

paint making it possible to sew a skirt that shimmers with light based on your movements or to draw yourself a paper piano that really plays. Crafts like these can be used as educational tools at the same time they let tech newbies exercise their creativity.

One of the most exciting aspects of the current crafting climate is the warmness of the various crafting communities. *Ravelry* is just one example among many: there's Instructables .com, countless kids' science and crafting sites, magazines like *Craft* and *Bust,* and marketplaces like Etsy that showcase the geek/craft connection. By and large, crafting communities both online and off—helped along by websites like Meetup .com, which helps connect local people with similar hobbies and interests—are a very welcoming bunch, with no barrier to entry. Part of that likely has to do with so many of us who are geeks to begin with. We know what it's like to be on the outside, and finally finding a community of like-minded folks can be a lovely experience.

And that's not to mention that we're sharing these skills with our kids. Many a Geek Mom among us has passed her love of quilting or feltmaking or lampworking beads on to her kids, or simply showed them how to upcycle seemingly useless scraps into household decor. Many of our own mothers somehow missed the crafting train, opting for store-bought and mass-produced items. But in spite of a missed generation or so, and judging by what our own kids are doing, I'd say Geek Moms are more than making up for it.

The History of Handiwork

Today, crafters are rediscovering lost arts, learning crafts such as embroidery, needlepoint, knitting, and crochet en masse. Historically, these crafts have been in the realm of women, but today that's changing. Many men are also now enthusiastically taking up their crochet hooks and knitting needles, creating items both functional and interesting.

As with most inventions, crafts originated through necessity, generating utilitarian goods. The makers would create something to meet a need. But almost as quickly, they started using these skills to create decorative things, adding embellishments to plain items.

Different forms of handiwork originated at different times in history. Embroidery started in the ancient world, possibly even in prehistory, and became a frequently used art in Islam during medieval times. Embroidered items indicated high social status, and embroidery adorned handkerchiefs, shoes, tunics, slippers, and more. Embroidery was a cottage industry in cities, employing a respectable portion of the population.

In addition to Islam, embroidery was used for decoration in India, China, Japan, and Europe. Embroidery guilds were formed in medieval England. An excellent example of embroidery work from this time is the Bayeux Tapestry, which depicts the Battle of Hastings from 1066. It is about seventy meters long and fifty centimeters wide.

But as the Industrial Revolution started, more of this work was done by machine. Because hand embroidery was no longer a necessity, it was eventually relegated to hobbyists.

Knitting likely originated in the Middle East, later migrating to Europe and then the Americas. The earliest found knit examples are cotton socks made in Egypt around the year 1000. The socks were of a quite advanced pattern, however, indicating that knitting was probably invented some time before that. Only the basic knit stitch was used for early knit garments, with the purl stitch finally appearing during the 1500s.

Eventually, knitting schools in England were established, which helped the poor learn a trade. Perhaps surprisingly, men were the first ones to take on knitting as a profession. Knit stockings were quite fashionable in Queen Elizabeth I's day, not to mention practical in the cold, damp weather of the country, creating a huge demand for stockings for both men and women.

Scotland also employed many people in the knitting industry during the 1600s and 1700s. Sometimes whole families participated in the business. Ireland took up knitting as well. Distinctive color and stitch patterns helped set their styles apart. Fishermen often wore wool sweaters because the natural oils in the wool helped keep them warm and dry.

Just as with embroidery, once the Industrial Revolution began, much of the knitting work moved to factories, again relegating hand-knit items to hobbyists or cottage industries for specialized goods. One interesting counterexample, however, occurred during World War II. Since wool was in short supply, women on the home front would unravel unusable knit items to reknit into warm garments to be worn at the front.

Knitting declined after the 1950s and 1960s, only to be reborn within the maker culture in the twenty-first century. Unusual uses for knitting, such as toys and public statements, have appeared alongside more conventional sweaters and scarves. Men have also been taking up the craft, emphasizing that handicrafts aren't just for women.

Crochet became popular in Europe in the 1800s, when patterns were becoming available. It may have started out earlier, though, originally using fingers instead of a hook, possibly first showing up in Arabia, South America, or China. At first, crochet was typically done by the wealthy for creating decorative items. As time went on, however, crochet was usually done by homemakers, and by the late 1960s, it had grown into a popular hobby. Granny squares, brightly colored smaller pieces that were then combined to make blankets, were a popular item to crochet. The popularity of crocheting then declined, but now in the twenty-first century it has also enjoyed the same resurgence as knitting. The internet has allowed knitters and crocheters to more easily share

patterns and develop communities surrounding the fiber arts.

Many other types of handicrafts have been practiced over time. Nålebinding, or needle-binding, predated knitting and crochet. It is somewhat similar to knitting and involves passing a needle through loops of yarn. It is still practiced today in Peru and Scandinavia.

Macramé is used to create nets, fabric, and other items by tying knots. It was popular among sailors, who already knew their knots well. They would make items while out at sea, and then sell them when they got ashore. Macramé was most popular during the Victorian era, but in the 1970s, it seemed to be everywhere and has enjoyed a popularity ever since.

The internet is helping those interested in this recent crafting movement find one another, meeting up for conventions such as Maker Faire, or banding together on websites such as *Ravelry*. The documentary and book *Handmade Nation* highlight the recent rise in making things yourself. And with websites such as *Etsy,* people are making a point to buy handmade items as gifts and for themselves.

JANE AUSTEN'S REGENCY PERIOD

During the early 1800s in England, young ladies and women of a certain class were expected to be well versed and well trained in the finer things in life, such as music, art, and handicrafts or needlework. Usually taught by their mother or a governess, the female members of the class would do much embroidery, cross-stitch, or needlepoint. One of their early projects was usually a sampler, which allowed them to learn and practice stitches such as cross-stitch. Most projects contained the alphabet or inspirational words, along with designs, the name of the crafter, and the date of completion.

Girls would start learning these skills as early as age five or six, and would likely be proficient by age ten or twelve. With a finished sampler, a girl could demonstrate her skill by the quality of her stitches. When women sat together in the sitting room during the day, they often spent their time on this work, for charity or to ornament decor around the house. There was usually a basket of work to do, so visiting ladies could contribute to the effort.

To start your own kids on needlework, transfer a basic design or child's drawing onto some cotton fabric, and put it in a small embroidery floss. For the very young, begin by teaching them a running stitch, which they can then use to trace the design. Older kids can use a backstitch in the same way.

Encourage your kids to invent their own designs. The final results can be made into pillows or framed on the wall. Or, kids can embellish items such as pillow cases or handkerchiefs. For those that enjoy this activity, a needlework kit is a nice gift. Put together a kit with different-sized embroidery hoops, several embroidery needles, scissors, a selection of embroidery floss, a marking pencil, and some fabric.

• **Running Stitch:** a simple even stitch created by running a needle in and out of cloth.
• **Backstitch:** a straight solid line of even sitches created by bringing a needle up through the cloth, then sewing one stitch length backward on the front side and two stitch lengths forward on the reverse side

SEW YOUR OWN FELT MONSTER

Custom geeky plushies are a unique toy or gift. Make them for your kids, with your kids, or even with your grown-up friends at a stuffed-animal-making party. Re-create your favorite monsters or aliens, use geometric shapes, or even make amorphous blobs that look like nothing to anyone except yourself. Use your imagination, and have fun with it!

$5–$10

30 minutes

Age 7 and up

Easy

materials

- Thin cardboard or blank paper
- Pencil or pen
- Scissors
- Felt in various colors
- Needle
- Thread
- Polyester stuffing or dry rice, beans, or lentils
- Embellishments such as googly eyes, yarn, or buttons
- Glue (optional)

STEP 1: Choose a Design

Decide what creature or shape you would like to create. In addition to monsters, aliens, animals, and robots, good options include geometric shapes like triangles, circles, rectangles, trapezoids, and parallelograms. But be creative! Choose a design that appeals to your interests. I have even seen plush statistical distribution graphs.

STEP 2: Make Your Pattern

On thin cardboard or blank paper, draw your chosen body shape. Once it is sewn and stuffed, the finished plushie will be slightly smaller than your full-size pattern, so plan accordingly. Cut out the pattern.

STEP 3: Mark the Design

On your chosen color of felt, trace around your pattern twice. If you are using patterned fabric instead of felt for this project, take that into consideration when you orient your pattern piece for tracing.

STEP 4: Cut out the Pieces

Carefully cut out both pieces of felt, following your tracing lines. Then match them up, trimming any edges that don't quite meet.

STEP 5: Sew Your Creature

With your two pieces of felt together, sew around the edges of the shape with a needle and thread, leaving a gap large enough for stuffing. You can use any type of stitch you like; it will only add to your creature's unique look. Consider using a contrasting shade of thread.

STEP 6: Stuff and Close

Stuff the creature with your chosen filling. If your creature has sharp corners, start by putting just a small amount of filling in those areas first, then stuff the middle portion. Once your creature is as full as you would like it, stitch the opening closed.

STEP 7: Embellish Your Creation

Your general creature shape is complete, so now you can sew on buttons for eyes, or glue on googly eyes or felt shapes for facial features. You can sew another piece of felt as a "shirt" on top of your finished plushie to make it look like it is wearing clothes. You can add yarn hair, gluing or sewing it to the plushie's head.

STEP 8: Experiment with Options

Use fabric instead of felt. During step 5, put the right sides of your fabric together for sewing, leaving a small gap. Then turn your plushie inside out and continue the directions from there. If you then stuff your fabric creation with rice, you could also add lavender or other herbs to create a calming gift.

Add arms and legs. Sew together long strips of felt or fabric for arms and legs and then sew them into the seams of the main body.

Make your plushie three-dimensional. Sew three or four panels together instead of two, and create an extra panel to sew to the bottom. This makes for a more challenging project, but your plushie will be larger and more interesting.

AMIGURUMI

not your grandmother's yarn doll

Perhaps you're a fiber arts master who can crochet a granny square in no time. Or maybe baby hats with ears and chin ties are more your thing. Or perhaps you are still fairly new to the art and can only crochet a scarf. As long as you have a few basic crochet skills and tools, you can make amigurumi. This project will teach you how to make a small, basic amigurumi sphere, along with providing several suggestions for embellishment and project extension.

But how to begin? Amigurumi isn't the simplest of crochet projects, but once you get a feel for it, it won't be as intimidating as it may look. I recommend having some basic crochet experience before you start, but since most amigurumi patterns use one of the simplest crochet stitches, the single crochet, the concept isn't too difficult to learn. If you've always wanted to make dolls or other little creatures but don't sew, amigurumi can be the method you use to create your army of minions or your gaggle of geeks.

This project isn't meant to teach basic crochet skills, so if you have little to no experience, refer to some good instructions available online for free at places such as Lionbrand.com, FreePatterns.com, and The Knit Witch's YouTube channel clips. Watching videos is a particularly good way to learn to crochet, since it allows you to see exactly what happens while a stitch is being made.

Don't worry if your first amigurumi doesn't turn out as you had hoped, or it takes a long time to complete. Because amigurumi crochet stitches are much tighter than those in most other crochet projects, it can require more effort to add stitches. You may find it helpful to rest your hands between rounds. You will get a feel for it as you go. If the tight stitches are still too difficult for you to work, use a slightly larger crochet hook than recommended.

STEP 1: Crochet Your Amigurumi

Rnd 1: Make a slip knot about 8" (20.5cm) from the end of the yarn. This will give you an end to use to close any hole left when your amigurumi is complete. Chain 6 ending with a slip stitch in the first chain. You have made your starting ring. Place your stitch marker before the next stitch. At the end of each round, move the stitch marker up to your current place.

Rnd 2: Sc 1, inc around (11 sts)

Rnd 3: [Sc, inc] around to last st, sc (16 sts)

Rnd 4: [Sc 3, inc] around to last st, sc (21 sts)

Rnd 5: [Sc 4, inc] around to last st, sc (25 sts)

materials

- Worsted weight yarn in desired color, 3½ oz (100g), 220 yd (201m)
- U.S. E/4 (3.5mm) crochet hook
- Stitch marker for crochet (the kind that opens and closes)
- Dry beans and/or polyester fill
- Scissors
- Craft needle
- Notions as desired (buttons for eyes, embroidery floss for detail work, felt for embellishments)

special skills needed

Knowledge of basic crochet stitches and terminology

crochet abbreviations and definitions

st(s) stitch(es)

ch chain

sc single crochet

inc increase (two sc in one st)

dec decrease (one sc in two sts)

sl st(s) slip stitch(es)

Note: *You can use a larger or smaller crochet hook for thicker or thinner yarn, respectively, but your resulting creation will also be larger or smaller.*

Rnd 6: Sc around (25 sts)
Rnd 7: Sc around (25 sts)
Rnd 8: Sc around (25 sts)
Rnd 9: [Sc 3, dec] around (20 sts)
Rnd 10: [Sc 3, dec] around (16 sts)
Rnd 11: [Sc, dec] around, sc (11 sts)
Rnd 12: [Sc, dec] around, dec (7 sts)

STEP 2: Stuff and Finish

Stuff your amigurumi with beans and/or polyester fill, and stitch closed. Weave in the yarn ends. If you've used black yarn for this pattern, you now have a ball of dark matter (or, for any color amigurumi that you

have stuffed with beans, you are now the proud owner of a hacky sack). Keep your creation that way, or you can embellish or transform it into other things.

STEP 3: Embellish or Transform

Here are a few ideas for embellishing your amigurumi, or branching out into more complex designs.

- Outer space: Use white or silver embroidery floss with your craft needle to sew stars or asterisk shapes onto the surface. Use other colors of floss to sew on red giants, blue giants, or yellow stars like our sun.
- Alien: Turn your ball into an alien with antennae. With the same yarn used for the body, make a slip knot on your crochet hook. Chain 4. Single crochet 1 in the second chain from the hook. Slip stitch in the next two stitches. Fasten off and attach to alien where desired. Repeat for the other antenna. Add eyes to the alien if desired.
- Ninja: Make a ninja by crocheting two black spheres, one slightly smaller than the other. Stitch them together. Embellish with a silver throwing star and a felt mask.
- There are many other options for making creations of your own imagination. You can glue felt shapes onto the ball. Or you can use different colors of yarn to create base shapes for other items. Use white yarn to make a Calvin and Hobbes-style snowman. Use gray to make rocks. Or use natural-color furry yarn to have your own collection of tribbles. The possibilities are endless.

- Once you master this basic amigurumi ball technique, you can adjust it to make longer shapes, larger spheres, arms, legs, and other features and body shapes. Some other geeky creations that have been made in amigurumi are Yoda, Slave Leia, and other *Star Wars* characters; Adam and Jamie from *MythBusters*; Doctor Who and the TARDIS; Hello Kitty; and the *Lord of the Rings* cast.

Did you make a mistake? Does your alien have a bump on his head, or is your ball of sunshine a bit asymmetrical? The good news is that even if you have trouble with a stitch or two, your amigurumi will still look great. Just keep following the intent of the pattern. Any quirkiness you introduce will only make each creation unique.

WHAT IS AMIGURUMI?

Amigurumi is the Japanese art of crocheting little stuffed dolls or animals. The word comes from the Japanese *ami*, which means crocheted or knitted, and *nuigurumi*, which means stuffed doll. This craft fits in well with Japan's *kawaii* culture, or cute culture, which appeals to people of all ages.

SIMPLE CROCHET INSTRUCTIONS

To begin, you'll need to make the first loop on your hook, which is a slipknot. Make a loop shape about 8" (20.5cm) from the end (or tail) of your yarn and insert your hook into the loop. Gently tighten the loop (1). In crochet, the slipknot does not count as a stitch.

Hold the hook in one hand and the yarn in the other. Wrap the yarn over the hook from the back to the front. Use the hook to draw the yarn through the slipknot on your hook to make a chain stitch (2). Repeat this process to make as many chain stitches as called for in the pattern instructions.

To make a single crochet stitch, insert the hook into both strands of the second chain from the hook, wrap the yarn around the hook, and pull up a loop (3). You now have two loops on your hook. Wrap the yarn around the hook again, and pull the yarn through both loops on the hook to complete the single crochet stitch (4).

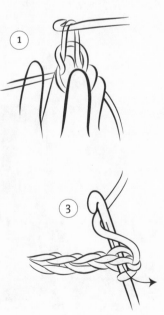

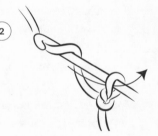

YARN BOMBING

If you think craftsmaking is a harmless hobby for quiet, unassuming people, think again. There's always been a thread of subversion running through the weave. Just look at Madame Defarge in A Tale of Two Cities, using her knitting to secretly record the names of her enemies.

Today the newest way to make a statement through craftsmaking is "yarn bombing." At the first World Maker Faire New York at the Hall of Science in Queens in 2010, fiber artist Robyn Love enlisted participants to knit or crochet woolen squares, which she stitched together into "flaming" streamers and hung from the tail of the museum's Titan 2 missile. Visitors were invited to write out messages of hope, which were pinned onto many of the squares. The squares were later made into afghan blankets and distributed to the homeless through Warm Up America.

According to the book *Yarn Bombing: The Art of Crochet and Knit Graffiti*, by Mandy Moore and Leanne Prain, the trend began in 2005 in Houston when a woman named Magda Sayeg knit a door handle cozy for her clothing shop. Soon the idea spread, and knitted "tags" began showing up on lampposts, outdoor sculpture, trees trunks, and bike racks. People began knitting sweaters for statues and replicating street signs in yarn.

Yarn bombing can be a playful way to make a statement, or just make a local landmark look cool. With basic knitting or crochet skills and a bit of yarn, you and your kids can practice random acts of beautification by surreptitiously making a cozy for Dad's favorite footstool, the big rock in Grandma's garden, or the gate to the playground down the street. For more ideas and inspiration, you can also check out *Craft Activism: People, Ideas, and Projects from the New Community of Handmade and How You Can Join In* by Joan Tapper and Gale Zucker.

NATURAL TIE-DYE SHIRTS

While in undergraduate school, I became fascinated with illuminated manuscripts and spent many dark hours in the library chasing old recipes for what could have contributed to the gorgeous pigments in the work of scribes of the Middle Ages. Reading these recipes was like discovering old alchemist's journals: ox gall, lapis lazuli, ashes, and even urine can be found among the ingredient lists.

Fabric is no less astonishing, with ingredients including bladders of certain sea animals, woad, and all manner of vegetable.

Curious components aside, I've always wanted to try my hand at natural dyeing techniques. Knowing full well that I don't have the capabilities to do something large-scale, I thought tie-dye would be a good place to start. I didn't need any huge containers for

dye creation, and the squirt bottle application meant it was easy for the geeklet to help out.

Note: Natural dyes are typically not colorfast. Even with the application of mordants (which help pigment bind to fabrics), like alum, which you can add to this recipe, they still will not hold up to as many washings, at least not like you expect with commercial dyes. The colors may also not be as brilliant. But hey,

$15

2 hours, plus more for setting

Age 5 and up

Easy to intermediate

materials

- 2 sturdy stainless steel pots; one small, one medium
- 2 beets
- 2 cups (500ml) pomegranate juice
- 2 tablespoons (10ml) each turmeric and mustard seed (ground)
- Vinegar
- Rubber bands
- Paint or chocolate squeeze bottles for applying dye
- Rubber gloves
- Plain white 100% cotton T-shirt
- Baking sheet

it's just another reason to use it again! You can always apply another batch.

I perused a series of recipes for natural dyes and came up with my own: bright yellow and muted pink.

STEP 1: Prepare the Dye

For the yellow: In the smaller container, combine 2 tablespoons (930ml) turmeric and 2 tablespoons (30ml) mustard seed, plus two cups (500ml) of water. Bring to a boil, then let simmer for an hour or until it has reduced by half. The end result will be almost pasty, and might separate slightly, but that's okay. Let cool and bottle.

For the red: Into the larger container put 2 cups (500ml) of pomegranate juice plus 1 cup (250ml) of water, and two cubed beets (you can grate them if you don't mind straining later). Make sure to use the rubber gloves when handling the beets. Simmer for one hour, let cool, and bottle.

STEP 2: Prepare the Shirt

After a good wash and dry to remove any potential detergents or chemicals, soak the T-shirt in a solution of half vinegar and half warm water for approximately one hour. Ring the shirt out, but don't rinse it. The vinegar will help the natural pigment bond to the cotton fibers.

A shirt can be prepared for tie-dyeing in dozens of ways, and the internet is an ideal resource. I just do a simple spiral. Lay the T-shirt flat and pinch the very center (both layers). Then begin to twist in one direction, until the entire T-shirt is a spiral. Secure with three rubber bands, separating it into six different sections (this helps with dye application).

STEP 3: Apply the Dye

Place the T-shirt on the baking sheet and put on your rubber gloves. With the squirt bottles, color the different sections in different colors. The mixtures will vary in thickness, so make sure the dye is getting into all the nooks and crannies. Since it's not as colorfast, I err on the side of more rather than less.

STEP 4: Heat and Wait

Once you're happy with the dye application, put the T-shirt (leave the rubber bands on) in a plastic bag. Microwave for two minutes. *Caution:* It will be hot, so kids should steer clear. Let the bundle sit for up to a day.

STEP 5: Rinse

After waiting overnight, I rinsed our shirt. The yellows were much brighter than I thought they'd be, since the initial dye is more brown than golden. The red turned pinkish purple, and orange where it hit the yellow. One good wash and the pink was faint, but the yellow was still quite vivid and has stood up to a half dozen washes so far. Hand-washing with very mild soap is recommended.

STEP 6: Expand Your Palette

Experiment with different natural dyes to get different effects. Black walnut and coffee work well for black and brown, as well as natural henna. Pinecones make yellow. I've heard of people using ground-up grass for green and blueberries for purple. You can also use fruit juice concentrates. It's a fun, cheap way to bring Mother Nature into the house, and the closet.

USING PHI IN YOUR CRAFTS

Fibonacci numbers. The golden ratio. If these don't remind you of high school or college math, perhaps they take you back to a childhood viewing of *Donald in Mathmagic Land*, that fantastic 1959 Disney video that taught us all how to play pool and create conic sections. Who knew that we could use this knowledge to add beauty and creativity to our crafts?

Fibonacci numbers start out like this: 1, 1, 2, 3, 5, 8, 13, 21, and then continue in this manner, ad infinitum. To calculate the next number, simply add the two previous numbers together.

Related to Fibonacci numbers is the golden ratio. They are related in that the ratio between adjacent Fibonacci numbers approaches the golden ratio. In other words, the farther along the Fibonacci sequence you go, the closer the ratio is to the golden ratio.

The golden ratio generates the golden spiral, the golden rectangle, and so on. A golden rectangle is one whose side lengths reflect the golden ratio of approximately 1:1.618, a number that is represented by the Greek letter ϕ (phi). The spiral is logarithmic, meaning the spiral gets wider with each ninety-degree turn.

Though both Fibonacci numbers and the golden ratio are mathematical concepts, they also turn up in a surprising number of places in nature. The number of petals on flowers is usually a Fibonacci number. The number of

spirals created by the seeds of sunflowers and the outside of pinecones and pineapples is a Fibonacci number. This is because Fibonacci numbers provide the most efficient use of space when packing in seeds and other parts of a plant. For its turn, the golden ratio is found in places like the Nautilus seashell and the length of the bones of the hand.

Making crafts using the golden rectangle is easy, since the object is simply to create or include rectangles with the fixed ratio of

1:1.618. Making crafts using a Fibonacci spiral is slightly more challenging. To do so, mark the center of your pattern, and place a dot slightly above it. Measure an angle of about 222.5 degrees, considered the golden angle, around the circle from your dot and place the second dot at that angle, but slightly farther out. The third dot will be placed 222.5 degrees around the circle from this second dot. Repeat until your spiral is the size you wish. Connect the dots in a curve. (This measurement is created by multiplying 0.618 x 360 degrees. Alternatively, you could measure 137.5 degrees for this project, which is 360 degrees minus 222.5 degrees.) In other words, if you want to make a clockwise spiral, place your first dot above the center at 12:00. Each new dot will be placed about seven and a half hours around the clock from the last one. Thus, your second dot will be where the hour hand is at 7:30, the third one at 3:00, etc.

Since the golden ratio and Fibonacci numbers can add significant beauty to a project while sneaking in some extra geekiness, mathematically minded crafters often integrate them in their work.

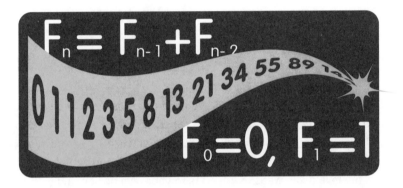

$$F_n = F_{n-1} + F_{n-2}$$

0 1 1 2 3 5 8 13 21 34 55 89 14

$$F_0 = 0, F_1 = 1$$

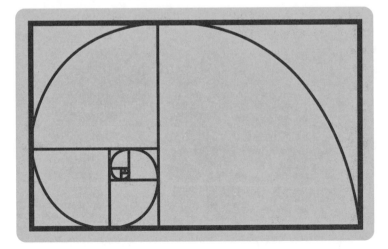

DIY BATTERY LIGHT-UP SCULPTURES

There's nothing more frustrating than a project that doesn't work. But sticking with it is one of the most important qualities a scientist, or an artist, can have. Luckily, geeks are made to persevere! For example, my kids and I have tried about four different versions of the classic "lemon battery" science experiment without finding one that could light an LED lightbulb. The way it is supposed to work is simple. Two different metals—usually copper and zinc-coated steel—are inserted into a wet, conductive medium—usually lemons. The wet medium breaks down the molecules in one of the metals, releasing electrons. The other metal happily receives them. And the flow of electrons creates electricity! It sounds straightforward, but somehow we could never get our lemon batteries to work.

Over the years I continued to look for the foolproof lemon-battery-type demonstration. And my search finally led me to a version that was not only small and simple, but artistic as well. I found it on the invaluable website Instructables.com, where a user calling himself "Madaeon" made little light-up sculptures using only some short pieces of drinking straws, wire, tissues, and a little lemon juice. Even these refused to work for us, but coming up with a nano-battery project that was foolproof became my obsession.

Finally, I came up with the version here. Follow my formula exactly, and I can guarantee success. Or try your own variation, and turn this art project into a science fair experiment! The choice is yours. The directions here are for a spider, with eight batteries for the legs that can light up two LED eyes. But

you can use these drinking straw batteries to construct any kind of three-dimensional structure you like—as long as you connect the batteries in a closed circuit. Add more batteries to your own design and you may be able to power three or more LEDs. Go wild, and have fun making sculptures using science!

STEP 1: Assemble the Buildable Batteries

Making buildable batteries isn't hard, but it takes a little concentration. To construct a spider, you'll need eight straws, each six inches long. Measure from the top down, so the bendable accordion-fold "knee" is included. Plug one end of each straw with a little hot glue.

Next, for each battery, cut one piece of copper wire and one piece of zinc-plated wire

$$$

$5 or less

2 hours

Age 10 and up

Intermediate

materials

- Bendable plastic drinking straws
- Uncoated copper wire, as thick as possible while still being easily bendable (about the thickness of uncooked spaghetti, if available)
- Galvanized (zinc-coated) steel wire, as thick as possible while still being easily bendable (used for picture hanging)
- Pliers/wire cutters
- Scissors

- Facial tissue
- Toothpick
- Hot glue gun
- White vinegar
- Disposable cup or drinking glass
- Plastic pipette or eyedropper
- Styrofoam bowl
- Electrical tape
- 2 or more LED lightbulbs, low voltage (2 volts or less)

about two inches longer than the straw. Then take a tissue and cut it into four equal strips the long way. If the tissue is multi-ply, separate the layers so each strip is one ply thick. Lay a piece of copper wire on a strip of tissue, leaving about one-half inch of extra tissue at the bottom. Twist the tissue around the wire until it is tightly wrapped, like a paper flower stem. Fold the extra tissue over the bottom as a cushion.

Lay a piece of zinc wire next to the tissue-wrapped copper wire so the ends are about even. Then take both pieces of wire and insert them into the straw, being careful not to poke either wire through the tissue. Pinch off any extra tissue sticking out about one-half inch above the top of the straw. Use the toothpick to push the rest inside the straw.

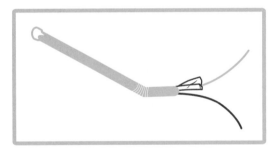

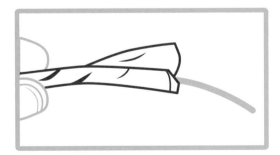

Pour some vinegar into a cup. Like lemon juice, vinegar is an acid that can conduct electricity. With the pipette, suck up some vinegar and squeeze it slowly into the straw. Let it soak into the tissue; if there are bubbles trapped in the straw, squeeze the sides slightly to release them. Fill the straw with vinegar almost to the top. Separate the copper and zinc wires by bending them apart slightly, then seal the top of the straw with more hot glue. Hold upright until the glue sets, about a minute. Do this for every battery.

STEP 2: Construct a Circuit

Electricity needs to travel in a closed, one-way loop called a circuit. The circuit for the spider consists of the eight batteries and two LED lightbulbs. The copper wire in each battery is its positive terminal, and the zinc wire is the negative terminal. You'll be connecting the negative terminal of each battery to the positive terminal of the next in a series. Each drinking straw battery gives off a little less than one volt of electricity; when you connect them in a series, the voltages are added up. If you used LEDs that run on two volts or so, your eight battery legs should be more than enough to produce some light. Only a portion of the energy makes it through the wires, however, so there's no need to worry about overloading the circuit!

Start building the spider's circuit by taking the copper wire from one battery, holding it next to the zinc wire of the next so that the ends are even, and twisting the wires together tightly. Bend any extra wires back toward the batteries and squeeze the extra wire together with the pliers to flatten it. This ensures a good connection and keeps things neat. Then add another battery the same way, until you have four batteries in a row. Set the first group aside, and make a second set of four batteries. When you are done, connect the two sets of batteries by taking the loose copper wire from one set and overlapping it with the zinc wire from the other so the ends are facing opposite directions. Twist the two wires together securely.

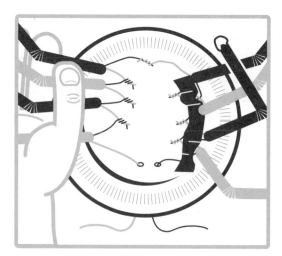

STEP 3: Finish the Spider Body

The body for this drinking-straw spider is an upside-down Styrofoam bowl. Tape the legs inside the bowl as shown. Then poke the loose wires through the bowl so they stick out where you want the eyes to go. (Use a pencil point to make a hole if necessary.) To make it stand like a spider, bend the legs at the "knees" as desired.

Now it's time to add the LEDs. LEDs, or light-emitting diodes, are one-way electrical components. They only work if wired to the circuit in the right direction. (The electronic jewelry project later in this chapter has more info on LEDs.) To find the negative wire, or lead, of an LED, look for a flat spot on the plastic dome. Most LEDs also have a positive lead that's longer than the negative. If you still can't tell which is which, just try hooking up one LED at a time. If it doesn't light, flip it around. (If it *still* doesn't light, make sure that all the wires are connected the right way, or try a different LED.)

Connect the two LEDs by twisting the positive lead of one together with the negative lead of the other. Then connect the remaining negative lead to the copper wire. You can poke the middle two leads through the bowl and tape them on the inside, to hold the LEDs in place. Take the last remaining lead and the last remaining wire. Bend them slightly so they are easy to connect and disconnect; you can twist them together loosely. This will be your on/off switch. Test the circuit by connecting these two pieces, and see the spider's eyes glow! Your sculpture should last at least a day before the energy in your drinking straw batteries is used up.

STEP 4: Try a Variation

For other types of sculptures, you can also make the batteries so that one wire sticks out the bottom. And you can make these any length you like. Instead of plugging up one end of the straw first, insert just the tissue-wrapped copper wire so the bottom doesn't quite reach the end of the straw and the top is sticking out. Use hot glue to seal the top. Turn the straw over, insert the zinc-coated wire into the other end, add the vinegar and seal as before. Connect the batteries together in a closed circuit as before, by twisting the copper wire of one to the zinc-coated wire of another. Bend the straws at the wire "joints" into any shape you want, attaching LEDs wherever you feel like it.

PAINTING WITH POLARIZED LIGHT

I don't think it's possible to be an artist without learning something about science. No matter what the medium, all artists become researchers when they begin experimenting with their materials and observing the way things like gravity and atmosphere affect their representations of the world or their imagination. Here's a project that works because of the mysterious properties of electromagnetic radiation in the visible spectrum. You'll need special glasses to get the full effect of these dazzling polarized light pictures.

Light waves, like most forms of radiation, generally vibrate in all directions as they travel. But you can use a polarizing filter to let only the light waves vibrating in one particular orientation pass through. Most physics textbooks tell you to think of the filter as a picket fence: only the waves that are straight up and down will be able to pass through the vertical gaps between the slats. If you crossed one piece of picket fence with another going side to side, hardly any light would be able to get through at all. But the analogy breaks down when you add a third filter diagonally in between the horizontal and the vertical slats—instead of blocking out even more light, the third filter lets the light through again! That's because the middle filter changes the direction of some of the light, letting some leak through when it hits the last filter. (It all has to do with photon emissions and quantum mechanics, a fascinating subject that you might want to explore further with older kids.)

Certain plastics like cellophane also act as polarizing light filters. When a light wave passes through the cellophane, the light bends. But the light going in one direction bends more than the light traveling in the other direction. This splits the unpolarized light into two separate waves, each polarized in a different direction. You can't see this happening under normal conditions, but when you put the cellophane between two polarized light filters (or one filter and a source of polarized light), the waves bounce off each other and produce a rainbow of different colors, depending on what angle you view them from. That's how you can magically create a multihued collage using nothing but a gray polarized filter, clear tape, and polarized white light!

STEP 1: Draw Your Design

You can use any kind of clear plastic or glass surface as a "canvas" for your

$$$

$5 or less

30 minutes

Age 3 and up

Easy

materials

- Thin permanent marker
- Bent acrylic picture frames (or Plexiglas or glass see-through frames)
- Polarized sunglasses or 3D movie glasses
- Clear cellophane tape (not the cloudy-looking "magic" kind; packing tape works)
- Recycled cellophane packaging or roll of cellophane gift wrap
- Black construction paper or craft foam (optional)
- LCD screen (TV, computer monitor, or other LCD device; optional)

artwork. Glass and some plastics will remain clear, while others will add their own layers of color. Bent acrylic picture frames that can stand up by themselves work particularly well with this project. If you want to use recycled materials, look for stiff plastic containers like those for produce or baked goods.

Polarized light pictures can be abstract or representational. Use the marker to draw any design you want. Only draw the outline—you'll be coloring in the rest "magically" later. You can also leave some or all of your picture area blank, and just let the colors make the image appear and disappear.

STEP 2: Color in the Polarized Design

Let very little kids just layer strips of tape across the surface of their canvas, whichever way they like. (Make sure it's the clear stuff—"magic" tape that disappears when you rub it down won't work.) For bigger areas or more

intricate designs, you can cut shapes out of sheets of cellophane packaging or gift wrap. It's easier to see the cellophane while you're cutting if you work on a black "placemat" of construction paper or craft foam. Don't worry about keeping the cellophane smooth as you

attach it to your canvas. In fact, the wrinkles and bumps add interest to the finished work. Every layer you add creates deeper and more varied colors.

STEP 3: Set Up the Viewer

For the movable filter, you can look through one lens of a pair of polarized sunglasses or 3D glasses. The newest 3D glasses use circular polarization, which means they won't change color if you rotate them. You can buy linear polarized 3D glasses with cardboard frames from rainbowsymphonystore .com for only a few dollars, including shipping. Cut the cardboard frame in half right through the nosepiece and you will have two filters. Use the earpiece as a handle.

You can see the colored image by placing one filter in front of the artwork and one behind. But it's more dramatic to light up your picture with polarized light. An LCD screen, such as a flatscreen computer monitor or laptop screen, makes an excellent light. To make the screen entirely white, open a blank word-processing document and set it to full-screen view.

Place the stand-up picture frame in front of the screen, or lean or hold your picture in front of it. Then hold up one polarized lens between your eye and the artwork. Slowly rotate the lens to see your picture "move" and change colors—all thanks to the magic of science!

BOB ROSS: HAPPY CLOUDS!

Name: Bob Ross **// Lived:** October 29, 1942–July 4, 1995 **// Occupation:** Painter, Art Instructor, Television personality **// Known for:** Inspiring the masses to quickly paint happy clouds and majestic mountains

Bob Ross, complete with poofy hair and a soft, gentle voice, taught PBS viewers of *The Joy of Painting* to paint landscapes for over a decade, from 1983 to 1994. In recent years, he has become a geek icon. Perhaps he added some gentle whimsy to our childhoods.

Bob began his adult years in the U.S. Air Force, yelling at soldiers to make their beds and shine their shoes. During his time in the service, he began painting and soon realized he could make a better living doing that than by staying in the military. He studied under William Alexander, who taught him a wet-on-wet painting technique that influenced his signature style.

Bob used this painting method to create layers of paint to form a picture. The lower layers didn't have much form, but then upper layers added more detail to make trees, streams, mountains, and clouds suddenly appear. The landscapes, which he is famous for painting quickly, were inspired by his time stationed in Alaska.

The belief that everyone had some amount of artistic talent was key to his teaching. He emphasized that it just took practice and instruction to allow it to come out. Any mistakes were considered to be "happy accidents."

Bob died at the young age of fifty-two from lymphoma. Those of us left behind can still learn from him, since all his television shows and his line of art supplies are available at BobRoss.com.

Bob Ross taught us that painting is fun, and that clouds and trees are happy. I, for one, was entranced while listening to and watching *The Joy of Painting* as a child. I had a love of art, but no real talent in it. Bob gave me hope and inspiration to give it a try anyway. My clouds and trees weren't as happy as his, but they did look better than they would have without his guidance.

UPCYCLE ELECTRONIC COMPONENTS INTO ELECTRIFYING ACCESSORIES

geeky beaded designs

I love making things from found objects. The first time I saw jewelry made from electronic components, I knew I'd have to try it for myself. But one thing I quickly discovered is that if you want to reuse parts clipped off printed circuit boards, it helps to know how to solder metal parts together. I'm still a newbie in that department, so I took the easy way out and bought a three-pound "grab bag" of assorted unused electronics parts from jameco.com, with handy wires still intact, for around $20. From that—and my collection of assorted beads left over from numerous other projects—I was able to construct several rings, necklaces, earrings, dangly charms, and more.

Of course, part of the fun of putting together electronic component jewelry is thinking up new ways to use and combine what you've got on hand. And I've learned that just a few simple techniques are all you need to start converting components into beading supplies. For more ideas and inspiration, check out the electronic jewelry designs on sites like techcycled.com or shops like digiBling on Etsy.com. Depending on your patience and fine motor skills, both you and your kids should be able to put together great-looking jewelry in just an afternoon with only a few basic beading tools and accessories!

$30 or less

1-2 hours

Age 10 and up

Easy to intermediate

materials

- Electronic components (see directions for details)
- Beads in various sizes, as desired
- Wire, cord, elastic, earring wires, clasps, crimps, jump rings, and other beading accessories, as desired
- Round-nose pliers
- Needle-nose pliers

special skills needed

Soldering and desoldering ability is helpful, but not required

risk factor

Watch out for components containing mercury or other hazardous materials; dispose of them according to the rules of your community. Don't open devices that may store a charge. (For tips on safely dismantling old devices, see Unscrewed: Salvage and Reuse Motors, Gears, Switches, and More from Your Old Electronics *by Ed Sobey.)*

STEP 1: What Do These Parts Do, Anyway?

You may be designing jewelry and not circuit boards, but it's still fun to learn what all those electronic components are really for. Here's a quick rundown on the most common pieces:

- **Resistors:** A resistor reduces the flow of electricity so you don't fry delicate components in a circuit. It's usually about the size and shape of a grain of rice, with wires coming out either end. Resistors can be found in a range of shiny finishes, including beige, foam green, and sky blue, and most have colorful stripes around their middle. Those bars aren't for decoration; they're a code to tell you the rating of that resistor.

- **Capacitors:** A capacitor stores energy, something like a rechargeable battery. It can be used with solar cells to collect electricity slowly and release it quickly, or to absorb surges and keep energy levels constant. Capacitors usually look like tiny barrels with two wires coming out the bottom, but they can also be found in small ovals and dime-sized discs. Their colors can span the rainbow, making them popular with electronic jewelry designers and fans.

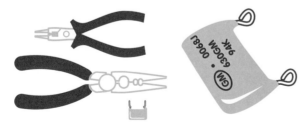

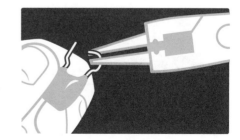

- **LEDs:** An LED, or light-emitting diode, is a powerful and efficient kind of lightbulb. Instead of a filament that heats up, inside the tiny plastic dome of an LED is a silver-colored cat's whisker— an ultrathin wire that almost spans a small gap between slightly larger pieces of metal. When electrons jump across the gap, they give off short bursts of light. The color of the light depends on the energy level and can be different from the color of the dome. LEDs are used wherever low-energy light is needed. For this project, we'll be using LEDs for their shiny jewel-like beauty.

STEP 2: Beading with Components: The Basics

If you've never done beading, the one simple technique you need to know is how to make a loop. With a short wire, take your needle-nose pliers and bend it out sideways, ninety degrees from the direction you want the loop to go. Then put those pliers down and grasp the tip of the wire with the round-nose pliers. Carefully rotate the pliers so the wire curls itself around one of the barrels. Keep rotating until the loop is closed with as small a gap as possible.

If the wire is longer, you can wrap any extra around the straight part for added strength. Start the loop the same way as before, but stop curling halfway. Slip the wire through the piece you're connecting it to. Then complete the loop, and start winding the extra around the remaining straight piece of wire like the end of a noose. Make sure the end is tucked in neatly so it won't catch on skin or clothing.

You can use this same curling technique to wind a wire into a tight or loose spiral "tube" that can hold the piece on a wire or cord.

Electronic components can be incorporated into wearable designs in a few basic ways. If two wires are sticking out from one side, you can curl them into loops or spirals and let the piece dangle from a cord, wire, or elastic string. If the component has wires sticking out on opposite sides, do the same by snipping off one wire and curling the other into a loop. Or make loops on the ends of both wires and create a chain by attaching the components one to the other. If the wire is long enough, you can slide beads directly onto it, making a loop at the end to hold the beads on. If using resistors, you can choose beads in the same colors as the stripes on the sides.

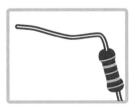

STEP 3: Some Ideas for Simple Designs

A quick LED ring is a great starter project, and easy enough for kids. Using the lightbulb as the "jewel," bend the wires around the finger you want to wear the ring on. Slide whatever beads you like onto the wires (for comfort's sake they should be small and all about the same size). If the wires are long enough to overlap, twist them together, letting the beads slide over the twisted section. If not, connect the end with a little piece of beading wire for extra security.

Or get creative with an odd-shaped component. In my grab bag, I found something called a crystal oscillator, which is used by microcontrollers to measure time. It looked like a flat metal can with one wire sticking out the top and two out the bottom. And it made the perfect framework for a tiny robot charm. I just slipped a large round bead on the top for the head, and two long "bugle" beads on each bottom wire for the legs. I secured each wire with a loop at the end, and hung it on a wire choker necklace along with a few other metal beads and components. Très cute!

Although you can build a necklace or bracelet completely out of electronic parts, my favorite look combines components and traditional jewelry elements. Don't be afraid to use a ready-made base, such as a plain chain or chandelier earring framework. Find them in your local bead shop or crafts store, or strip down and dress up old pieces you already own or find at yard sales or flea markets. With a little imagination and a good eye, you'll soon be making dazzling electronic trinkets that any geek would be proud to wear!

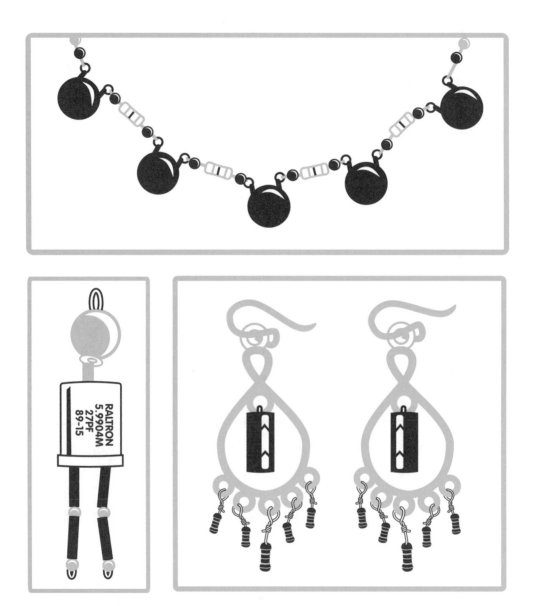

PROTECT YOUR TECH
(just for mom)

Many of our myriad portable electronics don't arrive on our doorsteps with their own cases. We usually have to buy those cases ourselves, and hope we end up with the right size, or the right one for our particular model. Cameras, mp3 players, cell phones, and portable gaming systems usually come with no protection whatsoever, and we hesitate to even use them until we have something in which to wrap them. But rather than spend a great deal of money on a store-bought solution, why not make your own completely unique soft-sided case?

$5–$10

1–2 hours

Adult

Advanced

materials

- Durable material for the outside of your pouch (main fabric)
- Soft material for the inside of your pouch (lining fabric)
- A thicker material to use as padding, such as cotton batting or fleece (make sure you have enough of all three types of material to more than wrap around your item the long way)
- Iron and ironing board
- Measuring tape or ruler
- Pen, pencil, or marking chalk
- Scissors, or rotary cutter and self-healing mat
- Pins
- Hair elastic in a complementary color
- Sewing machine and thread
- Chopstick or other turning implement
- Needle
- Button

special skills needed
Basic sewing machine skills, knowledge of sewing terminology

STEP 1: Prepare Fabric

If you intend to ever wash your pouch, prewash and dry all fabrics (but not cotton batting). Press with an iron.

STEP 2: Determine Measurements

Measure your device to find the dimensions to cut your fabric and padding. First measure all the way around the smaller dimension of the item that will be stored in the pouch (see Illustration 1). Divide this number by two and add 1½" (3.8cm). This will be the width measurement for all three fabrics.

Second, measure all the way around your item in the longer direction (see Illustration 2). Add 1½" (3.8cm) to this measurement. Also add the number of inches you would like your closing flap to be. The result will be the length measurement for all three fabrics.

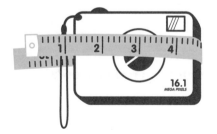

STEP 3: Cut Fabric

Using your ruler or other measuring device, measure and mark the length and width dimensions for the pouch on all three fabrics. Cut them out.

STEP 4: Attach Elastic

In the middle of the width edge (the smaller dimension) of the right side of the lining fabric, pin your hair elastic ¼" (6mm) from the edge, making sure the loop is the proper size for the button you chose. Pin the elastic to the fabric so that the loop that will go around your button is against the fabric and the other end is hanging off the end. Stitch in place.

STEP 5: Put Fabric Layers Together

On a flat surface, place the fabric layers down in this order, starting with the bottom layer: padding, main fabric right side up, and lining right side down. Your elastic should be facing down, against the right side of the main fabric. Pin around the edges with all layers together.

STEP 6: Sew Fabric Layers Together

Leaving a 2-3" (5cm-7.5cm) gap on the short side opposite the elastic, sew around the edge of the fabric stack with a ¼" (6mm) seam. Trim the padding layer close to the stitching, being careful not to snip any stitches. Cut the points off the corners, again without snipping any stitches.

STEP 7: Turn Right Side Out

Through the unsewn gap, turn your pouch right side out, making sure the main fabric and lining fabric are showing after turning. Use a chopstick or other tool to make sure the corners are fairly sharp.

Flatten the layered fabric, smoothly and neatly tucking in the extra fabric along the unsewn edge. Press the edges, being careful to avoid the elastic.

STEP 8: Sew Pouch

Top-stitch across the entire edge that contains the unsewn gap. Measure your electronic device's long dimension (not all the way around). Then fold the top-stitched end toward the elastic loop end the distance you just measured, plus a little more, with the main fabric facing outward. Line up the edges and pin.

From the fold at the bottom of the pouch, machine stitch all the way up one side, across the edge with the elastic loop, and down the other side back to the fold.

STEP 9: Finish!

Fold down the flap, and where it hits the front of the pouch, sew on your button with a needle and thread. Now your pouch is ready to safely store your device!

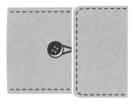

MAKE A WEARABLE MINI ABACUS

Long before transistors and microchips made pocket calculators possible, people were doing complicated arithmetic problems on the abacus. It's associated with China, but the idea of a counting board with beads originated in the Mediterranean and traveled east along the Silk Road. Several different kinds of abacus are still in use today. The Chinese *suan-pan* has two upper beads and five lower beads, while the Japanese *soroban* uses four beads below and one above. Then there's the Russian *schoty*, which has beads that slide sideways instead of up and down.

This craft will show you how to make a real working mini abacus in the Chinese style. It can be worn as a pin or hung on a zipper pull. Although it takes many years of practice to become a master at using the abacus, getting started is easy—especially for kids, whose brains often seem more open to new ways of thinking than their parents'. And while you'll probably still want to pull out your smartphone when you need to figure out the tip, it makes a great conversation piece for geeks who love math!

STEP 1: Start at the Bottom

To make this mini abacus, you'll be sandwiching the pins that hold the beads between strips of peel-and-stick craft foam, that soft squishy material that is so easy for kids to work with. Take the sheet of craft foam and cut six strips about ⅜" (9mm) wide and 2" (5cm) long. Take one foam strip and

place it horizontally on the plate, paper side up. Peel off the paper on the strip so the glue is exposed.

Take one of the pins and place it vertically with the loop end down in the middle of the foam strip. Place the second and third pins at either end in the same way. Place the fourth and fifth pins between the first pins, spacing them evenly.

Peel the paper off another foam piece. Position it over the first foam piece so that

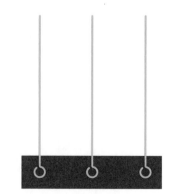

materials

- 1 sheet peel-and-stick craft foam
- 5 eye pins 2" (5cm) long (used for bead jewelry)
- 35+ small beads (large enough to fit on the pins)
- (optional) 2 interlocked chain rings (for a necklace or zipper pull)
- (optional) peel-and-stick pin backing
- 1 paper plate (to keep materials from rolling away)

the loop ends of the pins are sandwiched inside. Press to make a good seal.

STEP 2: Add the Beads

Slip five beads on each pin. The color of the beads doesn't matter, so mix them up and put them in any order you like. Make a center bar by placing more foam strips under and over the pins, leaving enough room for the beads to slide up and down. Then slip two more beads on each pin.

STEP 3: Finish It Off

Peel the paper off the fifth foam strip and place it under the tips of the pins, leaving enough room for the beads to slide up and down. If you want to add a loop for use as a zipper pull or necklace, don't seal the top bar with the last foam strip just yet!

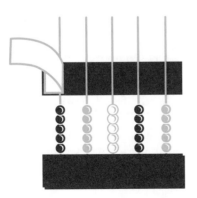

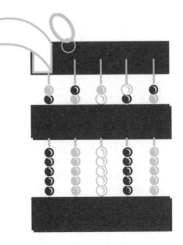

Take the interlocked rings and stick one ring on the foam between two pins. Peel the paper off the last foam strip and stick it on top, sealing in the tops of the pins and the ring. To make a pin, seal the top bar and attach the peel-and-stick pin backing to the back of the center bar.

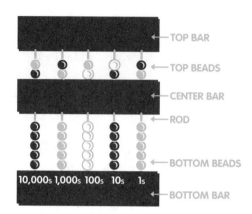

HOW TO READ AN ABACUS

In many Asian countries—and communities here in the United States—there are still special schools that train kids how to use the abacus. And the first lesson is learning how to read the numbers shown on the rods. It's really very simple. Just think of each rod as a place column. Going from right to left, you have the ones place, the tens place, the hundreds place, the thousands place, and so on. Beads come into play when they are pushed toward the center bar. So before you do any calculations, "zero out" the abacus by pushing all the beads away from the center bar.

The other important thing to know is that the bottom beads (sometimes called the "earth beads") are worth 1 each and the top beads (also known as the "heaven beads") are worth 5. So to show the number 205, you would push up two bottom beads on the hundreds rod, nothing on the tens rod, and push down one top bead on the ones bar. See?

It's really not hard, once you get started. To build up your skill reading numbers on the abacus, you can find apps online that will test you on your speed and accuracy.

HOW TO ADD ON THE ABACUS

First, zero out the abacus by pushing all the beads away from the center bar. Next, show the first number on the abacus. Then, working left to right, add each digit of the second number to the abacus. For example, to add 21 + 13, show the first number by pushing up 2 bottom beads on the tens rod and 1 bead on the ones rod. Then add the second number by pushing up 1 bead on the tens rod and 3 beads on the ones rod. The answer shown will be 34.

Here's where it gets complicated. If there are not enough bottom beads on the rod you are working with, use the top beads. For example, to add 2 + 4, zero out the abacus, then push up 2 bottom beads on the ones rod. Since there aren't 4 more bottom beads on the ones rod to push up, you will have to change the problem to "5 minus 1" instead. Always take away beads before adding. So you will push 1 bottom bead down, and then push down 1 heaven bead to the center bar. What you have left is 1 bead on top and 1 on bottom, for a total of 6.

If you've used all the bottom and top beads there are and you're still coming up short, you'll have to use beads from the next rod. So, to add 2 + 9, zero out the abacus and push up 2 earth beads to the center bar. Since there aren't enough beads on the ones bar left to make up 9, you will add "10 minus 1" instead. Push down one bottom bead from the ones rod. Then push up 1 bottom bead from the tens rod. You now have 1 bead on the tens rod and 1 bead on the ones rod, or 11. It may feel confusing at first (especially if you're older than a fifth grader), but keep at it and soon you'll be adding on the abacus like a pro!

ABOUT GeekMom

The *GeekMom* blog on Wired.com was founded in 2010 by senior editors Natania Barron, Kathy Ceceri, Corrina Lawson, and Jenny Williams as a companion to *GeekDad*, under the guidance of publisher Ken Denmead. Written by a staff of more than twenty core contributors and doztens of occasional writers, it has grown to become a true community of folks who share a variety of geeky interests, from sci-fi to cyberparenting to recycling. At *GeekMom*, mothers and other readers come together to be informed, learn new things that touch on their areas of interest, and find affirmation and validation for the choices they've made. If you enjoy geeky news, projects, and discussions come check us out at GeekMom.com!

GeekMom Blog Core Contributors

Rebecca Angel (rebeccaangel.com)

Brigid Ashwood (brigidashwood.com)

Judy Berna (justonefoot.blogspot.com)

Kris Bordessa (krisbordessa.com)

Sophie Brown

Ariane Coffin (wired.com/geekmom/autor/
ariane-coffin/)

Jennifer Day

Kay Holt (subvertthespace.com/kayholt)

Mandy Horetski (browncoatmom.blogspot.com)

Marziah Karch (marziah.com)

Kelly Knox (wired.com/geekmom/author/
kelly-knox/)

Amy Kraft (mediamacaroni.com)

Helene McLaughlin (wired.com/geekmom/author/
helene)

Sarah Pinault (mainemummy.blogspot.com)

Cathe Post (gtmermomv1.wordpress.com)

Kristen Rutherford (kristenrutherford.com)

Andrea Schwalm (flickr.com/photos/
ariaphotography)

Jules Sherred (juliasherred.com)

Ruth Suehle (hobbyhobby.wordpress.com)

Dakster Sullivan (wired.com/geekmom/author/
dak/)

Patricia Vollmer (vollmerdp.blogspot.com)

Nicole Wakelin (totalfangirl.com)

Laura Grace Weldon (lauragraceweldon.com)

Melissa Wiley (melissawiley.com)

Illustrator **Dave Perillo** was born in 1974, the same year Wham-O introduced the Slip 'N Slide . . . coincidence? In first grade, Dave revealed in his autobiography, *Me Book*, that when he grew up he would like to be Ziggy. This ambition was deflated by second grade when he realized that (a) Ziggy is not real, (b) Ziggy is completely bald, and (c) Ziggy wears no pants. While the thought of going throughout life sans pants was somewhat appealing, he decided to pursue his second choice, a career in art. Dave currently resides in the burbs of Philly, works as an illustrator, and believes that bowling is the sport of kings and that Swedish Fish is a seafood dinner. Find him at montygog.blogspot.com.

ACKNOWLEDGMENTS

The GeekMoms would like to acknowledge the essential contribution of our publisher at GeekMom.com, Ken Denmead, who first encouraged us to pursue both the book and the blog, and the assistance of each and every one of our blog's writers. We'd also like to say a special thanks to Kari Byron, who helped get us off the ground and made an invaluable contribution to Geek Moms everywhere.

Natania would like to thank her husband, Michael, first and foremost, for nourishing her geekiest desires and initiating her into D&D, as well as being a hobbit companion most days, and an adventurer on others; her son, Liam, whose imagination, curiosity, tenacity, and enthusiasm serve as continual reminders of the power of childhood and play; her mom and dad for embracing this whole geek thing and being her biggest fans; her sister for supplying her with years of geeking out on the Nintendo and in imaginary worlds; and the GeekMoms, GeekDads, and general geeks that she's come to know and love over the years on Twitter, Facebook, and at conventions. And last but not least, she'd like to thank vitamin B6 for making her second pregnancy tolerable enough for her to write her sections of the book.

Kathy would like to thank her homeschooling and GeekMom friends—particularly those who fall into both categories!—for their support. And her family, for putting up with her, and cooking supper when called upon, during the writing of this book.

Corrina would like to thank her families, both conventional and unconventional. That includes her mother, who always encouraged her writing; her husband, who purchased and put together a writing desk for her; and her four minions, the very best cheerleaders that a mother could have. Her unconventional families include her packmates, the cherries, the Glindas, the posters on YABS, and a special thanks to the chatroma BFFs.

Jenny would like to thank Abraham, her autodidactic learning buddy, one of the smartest people she knows, and someone who inspires her intellectually and personally (he also gives heartfelt feedback that's spot-on, better than anyone she knows); Alan, the inspiration and resource for several of her projects and activities, who is insanely smart and her longtime intellectual friend; her mom, the constant stable influence in her life, who has always loved her, supported her, and told her that she could be and do anything—she was right; her kids, who gave her life a meaning that it never had before, and are her most favorite people, ever; and Ed, who stood by her, encouraged all her personal endeavors, and loved her a long time—thank you.

INDEX